MASTER THE™ DSST®

Fundamentals of College Algebra Exam

PETERSON'S®

About Peterson's®

Peterson's has been your trusted educational publisher for over 50 years. It's a milestone we're quite proud of, as we continue to offer the most accurate, dependable, high-quality educational content in the field, providing you with everything you need to succeed. No matter where you are on your academic or professional path, you can rely on Peterson's for its books, online information, expert test-prep tools, the most up-to-date education exploration data, and the highest quality career success resources—everything you need to achieve your education goals. For our complete line of products, visit **www.petersons.com.**

For more information, contact Peterson's, 4380 S. Syracuse St., Suite 200, Denver, CO 80237; 800-338-3282 Ext. 54229; or visit us online at **www.petersons.com**.

ISBN: 978-0-7689-4449-5

Printed in the United States of America

10 9 8 7 6 5 4 3 2 1   23 22 21

Contents

Before You Begin

HOW THIS BOOK IS ORGANIZED

Peterson's *Master the*™ *DSST*® *Fundamentals of College Algebra Exam* provides a diagnostic test, subject-matter review, and a post-test.

- **Diagnostic Test**—Twenty multiple-choice questions, followed by an answer key with detailed answer explanations
- **Assessment Grid**—A chart designed to help you identify areas that you need to focus on based on your test results
- **Subject-Matter Review**—General overview of the exam subject, followed by a review of the relevant topics and terminology covered on the exam
- **Post-test**—Sixty multiple-choice questions, followed by an answer key and detailed answer explanations

The purpose of the diagnostic test is to help you figure out what you know—or don't know. The twenty multiple-choice questions are similar to the ones found on the DSST exam, and they should provide you with a good idea of what to expect. Once you take the diagnostic test, check your answers to see how you did. Included with each correct answer is a brief explanation regarding why a specific answer is correct, and in many cases, why other options are incorrect. Use the assessment grid to identify the questions you miss so that you can spend more time reviewing that information later. As with any exam, knowing your weak spots greatly improves your chances of success.

Following the diagnostic test is a subject-matter review. The review summarizes the various topics covered on the DSST exam. Key terms are defined; important concepts are explained; and when appropriate, examples are provided. As you read the review, some of the information may seem familiar while other information may seem foreign. Again, take note of the unfamiliar because that will most likely cause you problems on the actual exam.

After studying the subject-matter review, you should be ready for the post-test. The post-test contains sixty multiple-choice items, and it will serve as a dry run for the real DSST exam. There are complete answer explanations at the end of the test.

OTHER DSST® PRODUCTS BY PETERSON'S

Books, flashcards, practice tests, and videos available online at **www.petersons.com/testprep/dsst**

- A History of the Vietnam War
- Art of the Western World
- Astronomy
- Business Mathematics
- Business Ethics and Society
- Civil War and Reconstruction
- Computing and Information Technology
- Criminal Justice
- Environmental Science
- Ethics in America
- Ethics in Technology
- Foundations of Education
- Fundamentals of College Algebra
- Fundamentals of Counseling
- Fundamentals of Cybersecurity
- General Anthropology
- Health and Human Development
- History of the Soviet Union
- Human Resource Management

- Introduction to Business
- Introduction to Geography
- Introduction to Geology
- Introduction to Law Enforcement
- Introduction to World Religions
- Lifespan Developmental Psychology
- Math for Liberal Arts
- Management Information Systems
- Money and Banking
- Organizational Behavior
- Personal Finance
- Principles of Advanced English Composition
- Principles of Finance
- Principles of Public Speaking
- Principles of Statistics
- Principles of Supervision
- Substance Abuse
- Technical Writing

Like what you see? Get unlimited access to Peterson's full catalog of DSST practice tests, instructional videos, flashcards and more for **75% off the first month**! Go to **www.petersons.com/testprep/dsst** and use coupon code **DSST2020** at checkout. Offer expires July 1, 2021.

Chapter 1

All About the DSST® Exam

WHAT IS DSST®?

Previously known as the DANTES Subject Standardized Tests, the DSST program provides the opportunity for individuals to earn college credit for what they have learned outside of the traditional classroom. Accepted or administered at more than 1,900 colleges and universities nationwide and approved by the American Council on Education (ACE), the DSST program enables individuals to use the knowledge they have acquired outside the classroom to accomplish their educational and professional goals.

WHY TAKE A DSST® EXAM?

DSST exams offer a way for you to save both time and money in your quest for a college education. Why enroll in a college course in a subject you already understand? For more than 30 years, the DSST program has offered the perfect solution for individuals who are knowledgeable in a specific subject and want to save both time and money. A passing score on a DSST exam provides physical evidence to universities of proficiency in a specific subject. More than 1,900 accredited and respected colleges and universities across the nation award undergraduate credit for passing scores on DSST exams. With the DSST program, individuals can shave months off the time it takes to earn a degree.

The DSST program offers numerous advantages for individuals in all stages of their educational development:

- Adult learners
- College students
- Military personnel

Adult learners desiring college degrees face unique circumstances—demanding work schedules, family responsibilities, and tight budgets. Yet adult learners also have years of valuable work experience that can frequently be applied toward a degree through the DSST program. For example, adult learners with on-the-job experience in business and management might be able to skip the Business 101 courses if they earn passing marks on DSST exams such as Introduction to Business and Principles of Supervision.

Adult learners can put their prior learning into action and move forward with more advanced course work. Adults who have never enrolled in a college course may feel a little uncertain about their abilities. If this describes your situation, then sign up for a DSST exam and see how you do. A passing score may be the boost you need to realize your dream of earning a degree. With family and work commitments, adult learners often feel they lack the time to attend college. The DSST program provides adult learners with the unique opportunity to work toward college degrees without the time constraints of semester-long course work. DSST exams take two hours or less to complete. In one weekend, you could earn credit for multiple college courses.

The DSST exams also benefit students who are already enrolled in a college or university. With college tuition costs on the rise, most students face financial challenges. The fee for each DSST exam starts at $85 (plus administration fees charged by some testing facilities)—significantly less than the $750 average cost of a 3-hour college class. Maximize tuition assistance by taking DSST exams for introductory or mandatory course work. Once you earn a passing score on a DSST exam, you are free to move on to higher-level course work in that subject matter, take desired electives, or focus on courses in a chosen major.

Not only do college students and adult learners profit from DSST exams, but military personnel reap the benefits as well. If you are a member of the armed services at home or abroad, you can initiate your post-military career by taking DSST exams in areas with which you have experience. Military personnel can gain credit anywhere in the world, thanks to the fact that almost all the tests are available through the internet at designated testing locations. DSST testing facilities are located at more than 500 military installations, so service members on active duty can get a jump-start on a post-military career with the DSST program. As an additional incentive, DANTES (Defense Activity for Non-Traditional Education Support) provides funding for DSST test fees for eligible members of the military.

More than 30 subject-matter tests are available in the fields of Business, Humanities, Math, Physical Science, Social Sciences, and Technology.

Available DSST® Exams

Business	Social Sciences
Business Ethics and Society	A History of the Vietnam War
Business Mathematics	Art of the Western World
Computing and Information Technology	Criminal Justice
Human Resource Management	Foundations of Education
Introduction to Business	Fundamentals of Counseling
Management Information Systems	General Anthropology
Money and Banking	History of the Soviet Union
Organizational Behavior	Introduction to Geography
Personal Finance	Introduction to Law Enforcement
Principles of Finance	Lifespan Developmental Psychology
Principles of Supervision	Substance Abuse
	The Civil War and Reconstruction

Humanities	Physical Sciences
Ethics in America	Astronomy
Introduction to World Religions	Environmental Science
Principles of Advanced English Composition	Health and Human Development
Principles of Public Speaking	Introduction to Geology

Math	Technology
Fundamentals of College Algebra	Ethics in Technology
Math for Liberal Arts	Fundamentals of Cybersecurity
Principles of Statistics	Technical Writing

As you can see from the table, the DSST program covers a wide variety of subjects. However, it is important to ask two questions before registering for a DSST exam.

1. Which universities or colleges award credit for passing DSST exams?
2. Which DSST exams are the most relevant to my desired degree and my experience?

Knowing which universities offer DSST credit is important. In all likelihood, a college in your area awards credit for DSST exams, but find out before taking an exam by contacting the university directly. Then review the list of DSST exams to determine which ones are most relevant to the degree you are seeking and to your base of knowledge. Schedule an appointment with your college adviser to determine which exams best fit your degree program and which college courses the DSST exams can replace. Advisers should also be able to tell you the minimum score required on the DSST exam to receive university credit.

DSST® TEST CENTERS

You can find DSST testing locations in community colleges and universities across the country. Check the DSST website (**www.getcollegecredit. com**) for a location near you or contact your local college or university to find out if the school administers DSST exams. Keep in mind that some universities and colleges administer DSST exams only to enrolled students. DSST testing is available to men and women in the armed services at more than 500 military installations around the world.

HOW TO REGISTER FOR A DSST® EXAM

Once you have located a nearby DSST testing facility, you need to contact the testing center to find out the exam administration schedule. Many centers are set up to administer tests via the internet, while others use printed materials. Almost all DSST exams are available as online tests, but the method used depends on the testing center. The cost for each DSST exam starts at $80, and many testing locations charge a fee to cover their costs for administering the tests. Credit cards are the only accepted payment method for taking online DSST exams. Credit card, certified check, and money order are acceptable payment methods for paper-and-pencil tests.

Test takers are allotted two score reports—one mailed to them and another mailed to a designated college or university, if requested. Online tests generate unofficial scores at the end of the test session, while individuals taking paper tests must wait four to six weeks for score reports.

PREPARING FOR A DSST® EXAM

Even though you are knowledgeable in a certain subject matter, you should still prepare for the test to ensure you achieve the highest score possible.

The first step in studying for a DSST exam is to find out what will be on the specific test you have chosen. Information regarding test content is located on the DSST fact sheets, which can be downloaded at no cost from **www.getcollegecredit.com**. Each fact sheet outlines the topics covered on a subject-matter test, as well as the approximate percentage assigned to each topic. For example, questions on the Fundamentals of College Algebra Exam are distributed in the following way: Fundamental Algebraic Operations—20%, Complex Numbers—4%, Equations and Inequalities—44%, and Properties of Functions and their Graphs—32%.

In addition to the breakdown of topics on a DSST exam, the fact sheet also lists recommended reference materials. If you do not own the recommended books, then check college bookstores. Avoid paying high prices for new textbooks by looking online for used textbooks. Don't panic if you are unable to locate a specific textbook listed on the fact sheet; the textbooks are merely recommendations. Instead, search for comparable books used in university courses on the specific subject. Current editions are ideal, and it is a good idea to use at least two references when studying for a DSST exam. Of course, the subject matter provided in this book will be a sufficient review for most test takers. However, if you need additional information, it is a good idea to have some of the reference materials at your disposal when preparing for a DSST exam.

Fact sheets include other useful information in addition to a list of reference materials and topics. Each fact sheet includes subject-specific sample questions like those you will encounter on the DSST exam. The sample questions provide an idea of the types of questions you can expect on the exam. Test questions are multiple-choice with one correct answer and three incorrect choices.

The fact sheet also includes information about the number of credit hours ACE has recommended be awarded by colleges for a passing DSST exam score. However, you should keep in mind that not all universities and colleges adhere to the ACE recommendation for DSST credit hours. Some institutions require DSST exam scores higher than the minimum score recommended by ACE. Once you have acquired appropriate reference materials and you have the outline provided on the fact sheet, you are ready to start studying, which is where this book can help.

TEST DAY

After reviewing the material and taking practice tests, you are finally ready to take your DSST exam. Follow these tips for a successful test day experience.

1. **Arrive on time.** Not only is it courteous to arrive on time to the DSST testing facility, but it also allows plenty of time for you to take care of check-in procedures and settle into your surroundings.
2. **Bring identification.** DSST test facilities require that candidates bring a valid government-issued identification card with a current photo and signature. Acceptable forms of identification include a current driver's license, passport, military identification card, or state-issued identification card. Individuals who fail to bring proper identification to the DSST testing facility will not be allowed to take an exam.
3. **Bring the right supplies.** If your exam requires the use of a calculator, you may bring a calculator that meets the specifications. For paper-based exams, you may also bring No. 2 pencils with an eraser and black ballpoint pens. Regardless of the exam methodology, you are NOT allowed to bring reference or study materials, scratch paper, or electronics such as cell phones, personal handheld devices, cameras, alarm wrist watches, or tape recorders to the testing center.
4. **Take the test.** During the exam, take the time to read each question and the provided answers carefully. Eliminate the choices you know are incorrect to narrow the number of potential answers. If a question completely stumps you, take an educated guess and move on—remember that DSSTs are timed; you will have 2 hours to take the exam.

With the proper preparation, DSST exams will save you both time and money. So join the thousands of people who have already reaped the benefits of DSST exams and move closer than ever to your college degree.

FUNDAMENTALS OF COLLEGE ALGEBRA EXAM FACTS

The DSST® Fundamentals of College Algebra exam consists of 100 multiple-choice questions covering college-level algebra topics such as algebraic operations, complex numbers, equations and inequalities, and properties of functions and their graphs. The use of a non-programmable calculator is permitted in this exam.

Area or Course Equivalent: Fundamentals of College Algebra
Level: Lower-level baccalaureate
Amount of Credit: 3 Semester Hours
Minimum Score: 400
Source: https://www.getcollegecredit.com/wp-content/assets/
factsheets/FundamentalsOfCollegeAlgebra.pdf

I. Fundamental Algebraic Operations – 20%

   a. Operations with algebraic expressions

   b. Operations with polynomials (including factoring and expanding polynomials)

   c. Rational expressions

   d. Operations with positive, negative, and fractional exponents

II. Complex Numbers – 4%

   a. Conjugate

   b. Basic Operations

III. Equations and Inequalities – 44%

   a. Linear equations and inequalities

   b. Quadratic equations and inequalities (including quadratic forms and solving quadratic inequalities)

   c. Absolute value equations and inequalities

   d. Systems of linear equations and inequalities

   e. Exponential and logarithmic equations

   f. Equations involving radicals

IV. Properties of Functions and their Graphs – 32%

   a. Coordinate systems

   b. Domain and range

   c. Operations of functions

   d. Inverse functions

   e. Linear functions

   f. Quadratic functions

   g. Polynomial functions

   h. Rational functions

   i. Exponential and logarithmic functions

Chapter 2

Fundamentals of College Algebra Diagnostic Test

DIAGNOSTIC TEST ANSWER SHEET

1. Ⓐ Ⓑ Ⓒ Ⓓ

2. Ⓐ Ⓑ Ⓒ Ⓓ

3. Ⓐ Ⓑ Ⓒ Ⓓ

4. Ⓐ Ⓑ Ⓒ Ⓓ

5. Ⓐ Ⓑ Ⓒ Ⓓ

6. Ⓐ Ⓑ Ⓒ Ⓓ

7. Ⓐ Ⓑ Ⓒ Ⓓ

8. Ⓐ Ⓑ Ⓒ Ⓓ

9. Ⓐ Ⓑ Ⓒ Ⓓ

10. Ⓐ Ⓑ Ⓒ Ⓓ

11. Ⓐ Ⓑ Ⓒ Ⓓ

12. Ⓐ Ⓑ Ⓒ Ⓓ

13. Ⓐ Ⓑ Ⓒ Ⓓ

14. Ⓐ Ⓑ Ⓒ Ⓓ

15. Ⓐ Ⓑ Ⓒ Ⓓ

16. Ⓐ Ⓑ Ⓒ Ⓓ

17. Ⓐ Ⓑ Ⓒ Ⓓ

18. Ⓐ Ⓑ Ⓒ Ⓓ

19. Ⓐ Ⓑ Ⓒ Ⓓ

20. Ⓐ Ⓑ Ⓒ Ⓓ

FUNDAMENTALS OF COLLEGE ALGEBRA DIAGNOSTIC TEST
24 minutes—20 questions

Directions: Carefully read each of the following 20 questions. Choose the best answer to each question and fill in the corresponding circle on the answer sheet. The Answer Key and Explanations can be found following this Diagnostic Test.

---

1. $(5 + 3i)(5 - 3i) =$

  A. 4
  B. 16
  C. $34 - 30i$
  D. 34

2. Find the function of the line that goes through the origin with a slope of 3.

  A. $f(x) = 0$
  B. $f(x) = 3x$
  C. $f(x) = 3x + 1$
  D. $f(x) = 3x - 1$

3. A woman buys 8 cookies with a $10 bill. She receives 40 cents in change. How much does each cookie cost?

  A. $0.80
  B. $1.00
  C. $1.20
  D. $5.00

4. Which of the following is the domain in interval notation of the function f defined by $f(x) = \sqrt{3x - 6}$?

  A. $(-\infty, \infty)$
  B. $(-\infty, 2]$
  C. $[2, \infty)$
  D. $(-\infty, 2)$

5. Which of the following shows the rational expression in its lowest terms?

$$\frac{2x^2 + 4x + 2}{(x+1)^2}$$

A. 2

B. $\dfrac{2(x-1)}{x+1}$

C. $\dfrac{x+2}{x+1}$

D. $\dfrac{2(x^2 + 4x + 1)}{(x+1)^2}$

6. The point represented by the ordered pair $(-3, -1)$ would be found in which quadrant of the rectangular coordinate system graph?

A. Quadrant 1
B. Quadrant 2
C. Quadrant 3
D. Quadrant 4

7. Which of the following is the inverse f^{-1} of the function $f(x) = x^2 - 5$ over the restricted domain of the nonnegative integers?

A. $\dfrac{1}{x^2 - 5}$

B. $\sqrt{x+5}$

C. $\sqrt{y^2 + 5}$

D. $\dfrac{1}{\sqrt{x+5}}$

8. Which of the following is the sum of the polynomials $2x^3 + 3x^2 + 4x + 7$ and $4x^3 - x^2 + 12$?

A. $6x^3 + 2x^2 + 4x + 19$
B. $2x^3 + 4x^2 + 4x + 19$
C. $6x^6 + 2x^4 + 4x + 19$
D. $10x^6 - 3x^5 + 19$

9. If $f(x) = x^2$ and $g(x) = x - 2$ and $h(x) = x^2$, find $f(g(h(x)))$.

A. $x^2 - 4x + 4$

B. $x^4 - 4x^2 + 4$

C. $x^4(x - 2)$

D. $x^4 - 4$

10. Which of the following is the solution for q, given $\log(\log q) = 2$?

A. 10^{12}

B. 100^{10}

C. 10^{20}

D. 10^{100}

11. Find the solution to $x^2 + x > 20$.

A. $(-\infty, 4)$

B. $(-5, \infty)$

C. $(-\infty, -5) \cup (4, \infty)$

D. $-5 \le x \le 4$

12. Solve $|2x - 4| > 8$.

A. $(2, \infty)$

B. $(-\infty, -2) \cup (6, \infty)$

C. $(6, \infty)$

D. $(-\infty, 2) \cup (6, \infty)$

13. Which of the following is $i(5 - 2i)^2$ in the form $a + bi$?

A. $2 + 5i$

B. $-15 - 4i$

C. 29

D. $20 + 21i$

14. The relationship between Fahrenheit (F) and Celsius (C) temperature scales is given by $C = \frac{5}{9}(F - 32)$. If $0 \le C \le 100$, what are the corresponding values for F?

A. $-40 \le F \le 32$

B. $\frac{169}{5} \le F \le 32$

C. $32 \le F \le 230$

D. $32 \le F \le 212$

15. Find the ordered pair that represents the intercept of $2x + y = 11$ and $3x - y = 4$.

A. $(5, 3)$

B. $\left(\dfrac{6}{5}, \dfrac{43}{5}\right)$

C. $\left(\dfrac{43}{5}, \dfrac{6}{5}\right)$

D. $(3, 5)$

16. Which of the following solves the equation $2x^2 - 5x + 3 = 0$?

A. $\dfrac{-5 \pm 1}{4}$

B. $\dfrac{2 \pm \sqrt{3}}{5}$

C. $\dfrac{3}{2}$

D. $\dfrac{5 \pm 1}{4}$

17. Solve the radical equation $\sqrt{9q - 3} - 7 = 0$.

A. $\dfrac{10}{9}$

B. $\dfrac{46}{9}$

C. $\dfrac{52}{9}$

D. $\dfrac{4}{9}$

18. Factor the polynomial $4qr + 2sr - 2qt - st$.

A. $(2q - t)(2r + s)$
B. $(4rq + s)(2qt + s)$
C. $(2q + s)(2r - t)$
D. $2(2qr + sr - qt) - st$

19. Which of the following quadratic equations represents the graph below?

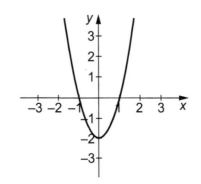

A. $y = x^2 - 2$
B. $y = 2x^2 - 2$
C. $y = x + 2$
D. $y = -x^2 + 2$

20. $5y^{\frac{3}{4}} \cdot 2y^{-\frac{2}{3}} =$

A. $7y$

B. $7y^{-\frac{1}{2}}$

C. $10y^{\frac{1}{12}}$

D. $7y^{\frac{1}{12}}$

ANSWER KEY AND EXPLANATIONS

1. D	5. A	9. B	13. D	17. C
2. B	6. C	10. D	14. D	18. C
3. C	7. B	11. C	15. D	19. B
4. C	8. A	12. B	16. D	20. C

1. The correct answer is D. Solve the equation using the rules for i and the FOIL method. Remember, i^2 equals -1.

$$\begin{aligned}
(5+3i)(5-3i) &= (5)(5) - 15i + 15i - 9i^2 \\
&= 25 - 9i^2 \\
&= 25 - 9(-1) \\
&= 25 + 9 \\
&= 34
\end{aligned}$$

Choices A and D are the result of FOILing incorrectly. Choice B is the result of calculating i^2 as positive 1.

2. The correct answer is B. We know the origin is $(0, 0)$. Therefore, using the point-slope formula we can find the following:

$$\begin{aligned}
y - y_1 &= m(x - x_1) \\
y - 0 &= 3(x - 0) \\
y &= 3x
\end{aligned}$$

The equation in choice A does not have a slope of 3. The equation in choice C has a y-intercept of 1, not 0. The equation in choice D has a y-intercept of -1, not 0.

3. **The correct answer is C.** To solve this problem, we need to create an equation. Let b equal the cost of each cookie. We know the cookies' total cost is $8b$. If we add the 40 cents, or \$0.40, to the total cost of the cookies, we will get \$10:

$$8b + 0.40 = 10$$
$$8b = 10 - 0.40$$
$$8b = 9.60$$
$$b = \frac{9.60}{8}$$
$$b = 1.20$$

Therefore, each cookie costs \$1.20. Choice A is the result of dividing the number of cookies by the initial amount spent. Choice B is the result of miscalculation. Choice D is the result of setting up the initial equation incorrectly with a $0.40b$ instead of $8b$.

4. **The correct answer is C.** For the answer to be real, the value under the square root must not be negative. Knowing this, we set up an inequality where the answer must be greater than or equal to 0:

$$\sqrt{3x - 6} \geq 0$$
$$\left(\sqrt{3x - 6}\right)^2 \geq 0^2$$
$$3x - 6 \geq 0$$
$$3x \geq 6$$
$$x \geq \frac{6}{3}$$
$$x \geq 2$$

The domain in interval notation is given by $[2, \infty)$, making choice C the correct answer. Choice A is incorrect since it includes values for which the radicand is negative. Choice B represents all values that make the radicand negative. Choice D features the same values as choice B but does not include the 2.

5. The correct answer is A. Use the distributive property to factor out 2 from the numerator of the fraction. Expand the denominator. Remember, $(x + 1)^2$ is $(x + 1)(x + 1)$. Factor the quadratic in the numerator and cancel out common factors. All of the $x + 1$ polynomials cancel themselves out in this problem:

$$\frac{2x^2 + 4x + 2}{(x+1)^2} = \frac{2(x^2 + 2x + 1)}{(x+1)(x+1)}$$

$$= \frac{2(x+1)(x+1)}{(x+1)(x+1)}$$

$$= 2$$

Choices B and C are the result of incorrectly factoring the quadratic in the numerator. Choice D is the result of factoring out 2 incorrectly in the numerator (not factored out of all terms) before factoring the quadratic.

6. The correct answer is C. The point $(-3, -1)$ graphs as follows:

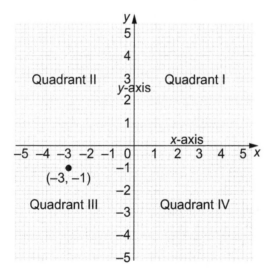

The point $(-3, -1)$ falls in quadrant 3. The remaining points fall into different quadrants based on the signs of the coordinates. Quadrant 1 has positive x and y coordinates. Quadrant 2 has a negative x and a positive y coordinate. Quadrant 4 has a positive x and negative y coordinate.

7. The correct answer is B. The inverse notation is solved by first assigning y to $f(x)$ and then switching y with x and solving for y, which gives the following:

$$y = x^2 - 5 \;\; \underline{\text{inverse}} \;\; x = y^2 - 5$$

Now solve for y:

$$x = y^2 - 5$$
$$y^2 = x + 5$$
$$y = \sqrt{x + 5}$$

Choice A is the result of a common mistake, which is $\dfrac{1}{f(x)}$.

Choice C is the result of switching the variables but solving for x. Choice D is the reciprocal of the correct answer.

8. The correct answer is A. Add the two expressions together. Rearrange terms and add coefficients of like powers of x:

$$\left(2x^3 + 3x^2 + 4x + 7\right) + \left(4x^3 - x^2 + 12\right)$$
$$= 2x^3 + 3x^2 + 4x + 7 + 4x^3 - x^2 + 12$$
$$= 2x^3 + 4x^3 + 3x^2 - x^2 + 4x + 7 + 12$$
$$= \left(2 + 4\right)x^3 + \left(3 - 1\right)x^2 + 4x + \left(7 + 12\right)$$
$$= 6x^3 + 2x^2 + 4x + 19$$

Choice B is the result of not adding the x^3 terms and dropping the sign on $-x^2$ in the second polynomial. Choice C is the result of adding exponents of like terms. Choice D is the result of adding exponents while combining unlike terms in the first and second polynomial.

9. **The correct answer is B.** To find a composite function, first insert $h(x)$ into the x of $g(x)$ and simplify:

$$g(h(x)) = (x^2) - 2$$
$$= x^2 - 2$$

Now insert $g(h(x))$ into the x of $f(x)$:

$$g(h(x)) = (x^2 - 2)^2$$
$$= (x^2 - 2)(x^2 - 2)$$
$$= x^2 x^2 - 2x^2 - 2x^2 + 4$$
$$= x^4 - 4x^2 + 4$$

Choice A represents $h(g(x))$. Choice C represents the multiplication of the functions, not the composition. Choice D is the product of h and f substituted into g.

10. **The correct answer is D.** Log is understood to be base 10, so we can solve by using the transformation rule $y = \log_b a \Leftrightarrow b^y = a$, where $b = 10$, $y = 2$, and $a = \log q$:

$$\log(\log q) = 2$$
$$\log q = 10^2$$
$$\log q = 100$$

Next, we use the law again, where $b = 10$, $y = 100$, and $a = q$:

$$\log q = 100$$
$$q = 10^{(100)}$$
$$q = 10^{100}$$

Choice A is the result of adding exponents when solving for q. Choice B is the result of squaring 10 and then taking that to the 10th power. Choice C is the result of multiplying exponents.

11. The correct answer is C. A second-degree polynomial inequality requires testing all possible regions of the solution. First, rewrite the equation so that one side equals zero:

$$x^2 + x > 20$$
$$x^2 + x - 20 > 0$$

Then, solve the problem as if it were an equation:

$$x^2 + x - 20 = 0$$
$$(x + 5)(x - 4) = 0$$

Thus $x = -5$ and $x = 4$.

Finally, test each region with a value from that region and determine if the original equation is true or false:

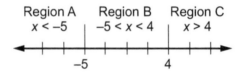

Pick a value from each region and test it in the original equation:

Region A = -6

$$
\begin{aligned}
x^2 + x - 20 &= (-6)^2 + (-6) - 20 \\
&= 36 - 6 - 20 \\
&= 10 \\
&= \text{positive}
\end{aligned}
$$

Region B = 0

$$
\begin{aligned}
x^2 + x - 20 &= (0)^2 + (0) - 20 \\
&= 0 + 0 - 20 \\
&= -20 \\
&= \text{negative}
\end{aligned}
$$

Region C = 5

$$x^2 + x = (5)^2 + (5) - 20$$
$$= 25 + 5 - 20$$
$$= 10$$
$$= \text{positive}$$

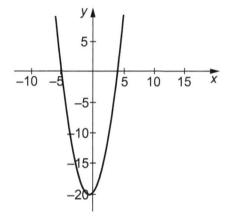

Values from Regions A and C are greater than zero. So the answer is $(-\infty, -5) \cup (4, \infty)$. Choice A includes values that make the inequality false. Choice B includes only one correct region. Choice D represents where the function is less than zero.

12. The correct answer is B. For absolute values, use the rule $a < -b$ and $a > b$ to eliminate the absolute value:

$$|2x - 4| > 8$$

$2x - 4 > 8$	$2x - 4 < -8$
$2x > 8 + 4$	$2x < -8 + 4$
$2x > 12$	$2x < -4$
$x > 6$	$x < -2$

The solution is $x > 6$ and $x < -2$, or $(-\infty, -2) \cup (6, \infty)$.

Choice A is the result of an algebra error and uses only the first inequality. Choice C includes only one inequality. Choice D features a sign error.

Note: For this type of solution, where the numbers go toward infinity, it is not correct to say $-2 < x > 6$. This notation should be used only for solutions like $x > -2$ and $x < 6$.

13. The correct answer is D. Using the rule $i^2 = -1$, solve the problem:

$$
\begin{aligned}
i(5 - 2i)^2 &= i(5 - 2i)(5 - 2i) \\
&= i(5)(5) + (-2i)(5) + (-2i)(5) + (-2i)(-2i) \\
&= i(25 - 10i - 10i + 4i^2) \\
&= i(25 - 20i + 4i^2) \\
&= i(25 - 20i + 4(-1)) \\
&= i(25 - 20i - 4) \\
&= i(21 - 20i) \\
&= 21i - 20i^2 \\
&= 20 + 21i
\end{aligned}
$$

Choice A is the result of missing the square on the second term. Choice B is the result of combining unlike terms. Choice C is the result of incorrectly calculating $(5 - 2i)^2$ as $25 - 4i^2$.

14. The correct answer is D. First, set up the inequality for F and substitute the equation in for C.

$$0 \le C \le 100$$

$$0 \le \frac{5}{9}(F - 32) \le 100$$

$$0 \le \frac{5}{9}F - \left(\frac{5}{9}\right)32 \le 100$$

$$0 \le \frac{5}{9}F - \frac{(5)(32)}{9} \le 100$$

$$0 \le \frac{5F - 160}{9} \le 100$$

$$0(9) \le 5F - 160 \le 100(9)$$

$$0 \le 5F - 160 \le 900$$

$$0 + 160 \le 5F \le 900 + 160$$

$$\frac{160}{5} \le F \le \frac{1{,}060}{5}$$

$$32 \le F \le 212$$

You can also solve this type of problem by breaking it into two inequalities and solving $0 \le \frac{5}{9}(F - 32)$ and $\frac{5}{9}(F - 32) \le 100$. The solution is $32 \le F \le 212$.

Choices A and B are the result of solving the wrong inequality. Choice C is the result of an arithmetic error.

15. The correct answer is D. First, solve for y using one of the two equations. The second equation will be used here:

$$3x - y = 4$$

$$-y = 4 - 3x$$

$$y = -4 + 3x$$

Substitute the value of $y = -4 + 3x$ into the other equation:

$$2x + y = 11$$

$$2x + (-4 + 3x) = 11$$

$$2x - 4 + 3x = 11$$

$$2x + 3x = 11 + 4$$

$$5x = 15$$

$$x = 3$$

Next, substitute the value of x into one of the original equations to solve for y. Either equation will work for this step. Pick the equation wherein the math will be the easiest to complete.

$$3x - y = 4$$
$$3(3) - y = 4$$
$$9 - y = 4$$
$$-y = 4 - 9$$
$$-y = -5$$
$$y = 5$$

Choice A reverses the coordinates. Choices B and C are the result of using the elimination method and subtracting 4 from 11 instead of adding, but choice C also reverses the resulting coordinates.

16. **The correct answer is D.** Use the quadratic equation to solve, letting $a = 2$, $b = -5$, and $c = 3$:

$$x = \frac{-b - \sqrt{b^2 - 4ac}}{2a}$$
$$= \frac{5 - \sqrt{(-5)^2 - 4(2)(3)}}{2(2)}$$
$$= \frac{5 - \sqrt{25 - 24}}{4}$$
$$= \frac{5 - \sqrt{1}}{4}$$

Choice A includes the use of b instead of $-b$ in the formula. Choice B just uses the coefficients. Choice C just features one of the solutions.

17. The correct answer is C. Use the steps for solving equations with radicals.

First, isolate the radical by putting it on one side:

$$\sqrt{9q - 3} = 7$$

Next, eliminate the radical by squaring both sides of the equation:

$$\left(\sqrt{9q - 3}\right)^2 = 7^2$$
$$9q - 3 = 49$$

Then, once all radicals are eliminated, solve the remaining equation:

$$9q - 3 = 49$$
$$9q = 49 + 3$$
$$9q = 52$$
$$q = \frac{52}{9}$$

Finally, check the solution using the earlier equation:

$$\sqrt{9\left(\frac{52}{9} - 3\right)} = 7$$
$$\sqrt{52 - 3} = 7$$
$$\sqrt{49} = 7$$
$$7 = 7$$

The value of q is $\frac{52}{9}$.

Choice A is the result of squaring only the left side after isolating the radical. Choice B is the result of subtracting 3 from both sides instead of adding. Choice D is the result of squaring only one side and subtracting 3 from both sides.

18. The correct answer is C. Group the first two terms and the last two terms, use the distributive property, and factor out $2r$ and t. $2q + s$ can then be factored out, leaving the solution.

$$\begin{aligned}
4qr + 2sr - 2qt - st &= (4qr + 2sr) - (2qt + st) \\
&= 2r(2q + s) - t(2q + s) \\
&= (2q + s)(2r - t)
\end{aligned}$$

Choice A is the result of mixing up variables when factoring. Choice B is the result of factoring only one variable out of some terms. Choice D is equivalent but is incompletely factored.

19. The correct answer is B. We know from the depicted graph that the equation must meet certain criteria. The graph crosses the x-axis twice, so the equation is second order, or contains x^2. Therefore, choice C is incorrect because it contains only a first-order x. The graph crosses the y-axis at -2, so choice D cannot be a solution. Choice D crosses at 2, and because x^2 is negative, it curves down, not up. The graph crosses the x-axis at 1 and -1. As such, choice A is incorrect if we test for $(1, 0)$:

$$y = x^2 - 2$$
$$0 = (1)^2 - 2$$
$$0 \neq -1$$

We know by process of elimination that choice B is the solution, which we can test with $(1, 0)$.

$$y = 2x^2 - 2$$
$$0 = 2(1)^2 - 2$$
$$0 = 2 - 2$$
$$0 = 0$$

20. The correct answer is C. Apply the laws of exponents to multiply the two terms:

$$5y^{\frac{3}{4}} \cdot 2y^{-\frac{2}{3}} = 10y^{\frac{3}{4}+\left(-\frac{2}{3}\right)} = 10y^{\frac{9}{12}-\frac{8}{12}} = 10y^{\frac{1}{12}}$$

Choice A is the result of ignoring the exponents, which must be added. Choice B is the result of an error when adding the fractions. Choice D is the result of adding the coefficients instead of multiplying.

DIAGNOSTIC TEST ASSESSMENT GRID

Now that you've completed the diagnostic test and read through the answer explanations, you can use your results to focus your studying. Find the question numbers from the diagnostic test that you answered incorrectly and highlight or circle them below. Then, focus extra attention on the sections within Chapter 3 dealing with those topics.

Fundamentals of College Algebra

Content Area	Topic	Question #
Fundamental Algebraic Operations	• Operations with algebraic expressions • Operations with polynomials • Rational expressions • Operations with positive, negative, and fractional exponents	5, 8, 18, 20
Complex Numbers	• Conjugate • Basic operations	1, 13
Equations and Inequalities	• Linear equations and inequalities • Quadratic equations and inequalities • Absolute value equations and inequalities • Systems of linear equations and inequalities • Exponential and logarithmic equations • Equations involving radicals	3, 10, 11, 12, 14, 15, 16, 17
Properties of Functions and Their Graphs	• Coordinate systems • Domain and range • Operations of functions • Inverse functions • Linear functions • Quadratic functions • Polynomial functions • Rational functions • Exponential and logarithmic functions	2, 4, 6, 7, 9, 19

Chapter 3

Fundamentals of College Algebra Subject Review

OVERVIEW

- **Fundamental Algebraic Operations**
- **Complex Numbers**
- **Equations and Inequalities**
- **Properties of Functions and Their Graphs**
- **Summing It Up**

College algebra covers material you may have seen before in classes in high school, such as solving linear equations or systems of linear equations. But it also includes a lot of additional topics like functions, their graphs, and their behaviors. Even if you have forgotten your previous algebra skills, do not worry! This guide is designed to take you through all the material you will see on the DSST and provide you with plenty of examples to help your understanding.

FUNDAMENTAL ALGEBRAIC OPERATIONS

Operations with Algebraic Expressions

Algebraic expressions are statements involving variables like x or y. The difference between an expression and an equation is that expressions do not include an equal sign and you don't solve them. Instead you simplify, add, subtract, multiply, or even apply exponents to them.

> **NOTE:** Use PEMDAS to determine the order in which to complete math operations. PEMDAS stands for **P**arentheses **E**xponents **M**ultiplication **D**ivision **A**ddition **S**ubtraction. Start by simplifying information inside parentheses, then simplify exponents. Next, complete multiplication and division (working from left to right). Finally, complete addition and subtraction (also working from left to right).

The most basic skill used when working with algebraic expressions is combining like terms. Like terms are terms with the same variable and exponent. The terms x^2 and $-2x^2$ are like terms, while $2x^4$ and $2x^5$ are not because they have different exponents. For any term, the number in front of the variable is called the **coefficient**. If there is no coefficient, it is understood to be 1. As an example, x can be thought of as $1x$.

Example

Simplify the expression: $2x - 4x^2 + 10 + 3x - 5x^2 + 1$.

As a first step, arrange these terms so that like terms are together. Note that constants (numbers) are like terms. Then, combine like terms by adding coefficients:

$$2x - 4x^2 + 10 + 3x - 5x^2 + 1 = -4x^2 - 5x^2 + 2x + 3x + 10 + 1$$
$$= -9x^2 + 5x + 11$$

We will see other operations with expressions in the next few sections.

Operations with Polynomials

Polynomials are expressions where variables are taken to an exponent (when there is no exponent, it is understood to be 1) and multiplied by a constant (coefficient). These terms are then added or subtracted to form a polynomial. Some examples of polynomials are $3x^2 - 2x + 1$ and $\frac{1}{2}y + 4y^5$.

Examples of the polynomial types are shown in the chart.

Name	Number of Terms	Example
Monomial	1	$2x^6$
Binomial	2	$4x^2 - x$
Trinomial	3	$5x^4 - 2x^2 + x$

Adding and Subtracting Polynomials

Adding polynomials is really about combining the like terms of the two polynomials, as you can see in the example below.

Example

Find the sum of the polynomials $-4x^3 + 2x^2 - 1$ and $10x^4 - 2x^3 + x^2 - 1$.

First, write out the sum and then combine like terms to find your final answer:

$$\left(-4x^3 + 2x^2 - 1\right) + \left(10x^4 - 2x^3 + x^2 - 1\right) = -4x^3 + 2x^2 - 1 + 10x^4 - 2x^3 + x^2 - 1$$
$$= -6x^3 + 3x^2 - 2 + 10x^4$$
$$= 10x^4 - 6x^3 + 3x^2 - 2$$

Notice in the last step, the polynomial was written with the powers or exponents decreasing. This is customary but not required.

Subtracting polynomials is similar to adding, but remember to always distribute the negative. Distribute the negative to every term in the second polynomial and then combine like terms. Notice in the following example how the signs change on the second polynomial when distributing the negative that separates the polynomials in parentheses.

Example

Find the difference of the polynomials $2x^5 - 1$ and $2x^5 - x - 2$:

$$\left(2x^5 - 1\right) - \left(2x^5 - x - 2\right) = 2x^5 - 1 - 2x^5 + x + 2$$
$$= x + 1$$

Multiplying Polynomials

How you multiply polynomials depends on the type of polynomials you are multiplying. You will change your method of multiplying depending on the number and distribution of the polynomials. Once you are done multiplying, you should combine any like terms in order to simplify your answer.

The simplest case of multiplying polynomials is multiplying two **monomials**. In this case, you just multiply coefficients and add exponents. We will explain why the exponents are added in a later section.

We will now look at each of the cases you may run across.

Example

Find the product: $(2x^4)(6x^2)$

$$\left(2x^4\right)\left(6x^2\right) = 12x^{4+2} = 12x^6$$

You can also multiply a monomial and other polynomials by applying the distributive property. In other words, you will multiply the monomial with each term of the other polynomial.

Example

Multiply: $(3x^2)(-3x^4 + 2x^3 + 6x + 1)$

$$(3x^2)(-3x^4 + 2x^3 + 6x + 1) = -9x^6 + 6x^5 + 18x^3 + 3x^2$$

Notice that $6x$ was treated as though it had an exponent of 1.

A special case of multiplying polynomials is when you are multiplying two **binomials**. To do this, apply the FOIL method. Let's walk through this with an example.

....

NOTE: FOIL is an acronym that stands for **First, Outer, Inner, Last.**

....

Example

FOIL the binomials $(x - 4)(x + 6)$.

Step 1. Multiply the first two terms:

$$(\underline{x} - 4)(\underline{x} + 6) = x^2 + \dots$$

Step 2. Multiply the outer two terms:

$$(\underline{x} - 4)(x + \underline{6}) = x^2 + 6x + \dots$$

Step 3. Multiply the inner two terms:

$$(x - \underline{4})(\underline{x} + 6) = x^2 + 6x + (-4x) + \dots$$

Step 4. Multiply the last two terms:

$$(x - \underline{4})(x + \underline{6}) = x^2 + 6x + (-4x) + (-24)$$

As a last step, you should combine like terms:

$$(x-4)(x+6) = x^2 + 6x + (-4x) + (-24)$$
$$= x^2 + 2x - 24$$

Let's look at one last example, without writing out each step.

Example

Find the product of $x^2 + 4$ and $2x^3 + x^2$.

Apply FOIL since these are two binomials, then combine like terms if necessary:

$$(x^2 + 4)(2x^3 + x^2) = 2x^5 + x^4 + 8x^3 + 4x^2$$

Sometimes you will have to multiply a **trinomial** and a binomial or even two trinomials. Remember that every term in the second polynomial must be multiplied by every term in the first polynomial. Basically, you must distribute every term of the first polynomial across the second polynomial.

Let's look at an example where the terms multiplied are written out.

Example

Multiply the polynomials $(x + 2)(x^3 - 8x + 1)$.

$$(x+2)(x^3 - 8x + 1) = x(x^3) - (x)(8x) + 1(x) + 2(x^3) - (2)(8x) + (2)(1)$$
$$= x^4 - 8x^2 + x + 2x^3 - 16x + 2$$
$$= x^4 + 2x^3 - 8x^2 - 15x + 2$$

Factoring Polynomials Over Real Numbers

Many polynomials are the result of polynomials having been multiplied together. Factoring is the opposite of multiplying. Factoring identifies the polynomials that were originally multiplied together. You should memorize these basic rules for factoring common polynomials.

Factoring Rules for Polynomials

$$x^2 - y^2 = (x+y)(x-y)$$
$$x^2 + 2xy + y^2 = (x+y)^2$$
$$x^2 - 2xy + y^2 = (x-y)^2$$
$$x^3 + 3x^2y + 3xy^2 + y^3 = (x+y)^3$$
$$x^3 - 3x^2y + 3xy^2 - y^3 = (x-y)^3$$

Factoring Polynomials of the Form $ax^2 + bx + c$

The basic factoring rules don't apply to every polynomial. A common case involves reverse FOILing, as shown in the next example.

Example

Factor the polynomial $6x^2 - 7x - 3$.

When asked to factor a polynomial, think "FOIL backwards" to solve. What values of $(ax + b)(cx + d)$ would arrive at the answer $6x^2 - 7x - 3$? For this solution to be true, we know $ac = 6$ and $bd = -3$. Also, we know that $bc + ad = -7$.

We know that 6 has factors 1, 6, 3, and 2. Also, 3 has factors 1 and 3. We first should try -3 and 1 for b and d, and we can try 2 and 3 for a and b. With some trial and error, we can arrive at the solution:

$$6x^2 - 7x - 3 = (ax - 3)(bx + 1)$$
$$= (2x - 3)(3x + 1)$$

Remember to check your solution by multiplying the factors out to make sure your answer is correct.

Factoring Out Common Factors

You can also factor polynomials by factoring out **common factors**. Common factors are factors shared by each term in the polynomial.

Example

Factor completely: $4x^5 + 16x^4 + 8x^2$

Each term in this polynomial shares a factor of 4. Additionally, looking at the variables, you can see each term also shares a factor of x^2. Factor out $4x^2$:

$$4x^5 + 16x^4 + 8x^2 = 4x^2(x^3 + 4x^2 + 2)$$

Notice that this is like undoing the multiplication of a monomial and another polynomial.

Rational Expressions

Rational expressions are formed when two polynomials form a fraction. Examples include $\dfrac{x+4}{x-1}$ and $\dfrac{2x^4-x}{2x^6}$. Operations with rational expressions are just like the operations used with regular fractions; however, you also must pay attention to variables.

Simplifying Rational Expressions

To simplify a rational expression, cancel any common factors shared by both the numerator (the top of the fraction) and the denominator (the bottom of the fraction) of the expression.

Example

Simplify the expression: $\dfrac{2x^2 - x}{2x^2}$

Be careful! You may want to cancel the $2x^2$ terms, but they are not factors. You can only cancel out terms that are shared by each polynomial. In the numerator, $2x^2$ cannot be factored from $-x$, but we can factor out an x from both polynomials. We can also do this in the denominator to simplify:

$$\frac{2x^2 - x}{2x^2} = \frac{x(2x - 1)}{x(2x)} = \frac{2x - 1}{2x}$$

In some cases, you may need to do more complicated factoring.

Example

Simplify: $\dfrac{x^2 + 3x - 4}{x^2 + 4x - 5}$

$$\frac{x^2 + 3x - 4}{x^2 + 4x - 5} = \frac{(x+4)(x-1)}{(x+5)(x-1)} = \frac{x+4}{x+5}$$

Adding and Subtracting Rational Expressions

In order to add or subtract rational expressions, you must use a common denominator just as you would with regular fractions. Then, add or subtract across the top of the fractions. When subtracting, make sure to distribute the negative to all terms in the numerator.

Example

Add: $\dfrac{x+1}{x-5} + \dfrac{x+2}{x+6}$

The common denominator here will be the product of $x - 5$ and $x + 6$. In this case, you will multiply the two denominators to find a common denominator.

Now use the common denominator to add the expressions. Notice that you multiply the top and bottom of the fraction by the missing part of the common denominator:

$$\begin{aligned}
\frac{x+1}{x-5} + \frac{x+2}{x+6} &= \frac{x+1}{x-5}\left(\frac{x+6}{x+6}\right) + \frac{x+2}{x+6}\left(\frac{x-5}{x-5}\right) \\
&= \frac{x^2 + 7x + 6}{(x-5)(x+6)} + \frac{x^2 - 3x - 10}{(x-5)(x+6)} \\
&= \frac{2x^2 + 4x - 4}{(x-5)(x+6)} \\
&= \frac{2(x^2 + 2x - 2)}{(x+5)(x+6)}
\end{aligned}$$

How much you simplify (for example, we did not multiply the terms on the bottom of the expression) will depend on the answer choices. Look at a question's answer options to decide whether to completely multiply within the numerator and denominator or factor out values as shown with the 2, etc.

Multiplying and Dividing Rational Expressions

To multiply rational expressions, multiply terms straight across as you would with simple fractions. This process was used in the previous example to find a common denominator. However, you can also use "cross canceling," which can save time when simplifying your final answer. Anytime there are common factors on either side of the multiplication symbol, you can cancel them out. Therefore, it is a good idea to factor as a first step.

Example

Multiply: $\dfrac{3x^2 + 3}{x^2 - x - 2} \times \dfrac{x^2 + 2x + 1}{3}$

$$\dfrac{3x^2 + 3}{x^2 - x - 2} \times \dfrac{x^2 + 2x + 1}{3} = \dfrac{\cancel{3}(x^2 + 1)}{\cancel{(x+1)}(x - 2)} \times \dfrac{\cancel{(x+1)}(x + 1)}{\cancel{3}}$$

$$= \dfrac{x^2 + 1}{x - 2} \times \dfrac{x + 1}{1}$$

$$= \dfrac{x^3 + x^2 + x + 1}{x - 2}$$

When dividing rational expressions, the first expression stays the same, but you will multiply it by the reciprocal of the second expression. You can't cross cancel until you have switched to multiplication.

> **NOTE:** A reciprocal is the inverse of a value or expression. For example, the reciprocal of 7 is $\frac{1}{7}$ and the reciprocal of $\frac{x+1}{3}$ is $\frac{3}{x+1}$. When you multiply a number by its reciprocal, $\frac{7}{1} \times \frac{1}{7}$, the result is always 1.

Example

Divide: $\dfrac{x^2 - x - 6}{2x + 1} \div \dfrac{x^2 + 7x + 10}{3x + 1}$

$$\dfrac{x^2 - x - 6}{2x + 1} \div \dfrac{x^2 + 7x + 10}{3x + 1} = \dfrac{x^2 - x - 6}{2x + 1} \times \dfrac{3x + 1}{x^2 + 7x + 10}$$

$$= \dfrac{(x - 3)\cancel{(x + 2)}}{2x + 1} \times \dfrac{3x + 1}{(x + 5)\cancel{(x + 2)}}$$

$$= \dfrac{3x^2 - 8x - 3}{2x^2 + 11x + 5}$$

Division problems can also be written as complex fractions. These are fractions within a fraction. For example, the division problem above can also be presented this way:

$$\frac{x^2 - x - 6}{2x + 1} \div \frac{x^2 + 7x + 10}{3x + 1} = \frac{\dfrac{x^2 - x - 6}{2x + 1}}{\dfrac{x^2 + 7x + 10}{3x + 1}}$$

Operations with Positive, Negative, and Fractional Exponents

Positive and Negative Exponents

Working with exponent problems requires knowing a few rules, as shown in the following table. Skill with exponents is critical to your success with college algebra, so solve many of these types of problems until you are comfortable with the rules.

Rules for Exponents	
Product	$a^m a^n = a^{m+n}$
Product of a power	$(a^m)^n = a^{mn}$
Quotient to a power	$\left(\dfrac{a}{b}\right)^n = \dfrac{a^n}{b^n}$
Quotient	$\dfrac{a^m}{a^n} = a^{m-n}$
Zero exponent	$a^0 = 1$
Negative exponent	$a^{-n} = \dfrac{1}{a^n}$
Inversion	$\left(\dfrac{a}{b}\right)^{-n} = \left(\dfrac{b}{a}\right)^n$
Fractional powers	$a^{\frac{m}{n}} = \sqrt[n]{a^m}$

Example

Simplify the expression: $\left(\dfrac{x^2 y^4}{x^{-1} y} \right)^{-2}$

Here, apply the rules for exponents within the parentheses and then apply the −2 power. Note that a variable with no exponent is assumed to have an exponent of 1:

$$\left(\frac{x^2 y^4}{x^{-1} y} \right)^{-2} = \left(x^{2-(-1)} y^{4-1} \right)^{-2} = \left(x^3 y^3 \right)^{-2} = x^{-6} y^{-6} = \frac{1}{x^6 y^6}$$

Fractional Exponents

Fractional exponents follow the same rules as other exponents. However, fractional exponents can also be written as roots (**radicals**). Radical expressions like this are those that use the symbol $\sqrt{}$ to represent roots of a variable. This is based on the following rule:

$$x^{\frac{m}{n}} = \sqrt[n]{x^m}$$

Example

Simplify the expression $\dfrac{x^{\frac{1}{2}} y^2}{x^{\frac{2}{3}} y^{\frac{1}{2}}}$. Write your answer as a radical expression.

First, apply the rules for exponents. Then apply the rule that $x^{\frac{m}{n}} = \sqrt[n]{x^m}$:

$$\frac{x^{\frac{1}{2}} y^2}{x^{\frac{2}{3}} y^{\frac{1}{2}}} = x^{\frac{1}{2}-\frac{2}{3}} y^{2-\frac{1}{2}} = x^{-\frac{1}{6}} y^{\frac{3}{2}} = \frac{y^{\frac{3}{2}}}{x^{\frac{1}{6}}} = \frac{\sqrt{y^3}}{\sqrt[6]{x}}$$

This expression can be simplified further. Since $y^3 = y \cdot y^2$ and $\sqrt{y^2} = y$, we can write:

$$\frac{\sqrt{y^3}}{\sqrt[6]{x}} = \frac{\sqrt{y y^2}}{\sqrt[6]{x}} = \frac{y \sqrt{y}}{\sqrt[6]{x}}$$

You can simplify these radical expressions anytime this occurs. The following table provides useful rules for working with radical expressions:

Radical Expression Laws

$$\sqrt[n]{a} = a^{\frac{1}{n}}$$

$$a^{\frac{m}{n}} = \sqrt[n]{a^m}$$

$$\sqrt[n]{a} \cdot \sqrt[n]{b} = \sqrt[n]{ab}$$

$$\sqrt[n]{\frac{a}{b}} = \frac{\sqrt[n]{a}}{\sqrt[n]{b}}$$

$$\sqrt[nm]{a} = \sqrt[m]{\sqrt[n]{a}}$$

$$\sqrt[n]{a^n} = a$$

These rules are demonstrated by the following example.

Example

Simplify the radical $\sqrt[4]{x^6 y^4}$.

Remember, $\sqrt[n]{a^n} = a$. By factoring out x^2 and rearranging, we can pull out xy:

$$\sqrt[4]{x^6 y^4} = \sqrt[4]{\left(x^4 y^4\right)\left(x^2\right)}$$
$$= \sqrt[4]{\left(xy\right)^4 \left(x^2\right)}$$
$$= \sqrt[4]{\left(xy\right)^4} \sqrt[4]{x^2}$$
$$= (xy)(x^{\frac{1}{2}})$$
$$= xy\sqrt{x}$$

COMPLEX NUMBERS

Complex numbers are numbers of the form $a + bi$, where a and b are real numbers and $i = \sqrt{-1}$. In fact, all real numbers are also complex numbers where $b = 0$. In the form $a + bi$ form, the a is called the real part and the bi is called the imaginary part.

Conjugates

The conjugate of a complex number $a + bi$ is $a - bi$. That is, it is the same number with the sign in the middle changed. For example, the conjugate of $3 + 2i$ would be $3 - 2i$. When you multiply conjugates, you eliminate the imaginary part (bi) and get a real number.

Example

Find $(5 - 2i)(5 + 2i)$.

Apply FOIL anytime you multiply two complex numbers:

$$(5 - 2i)(5 + 2i) = 25 - 4i^2$$

Now apply the idea that since $i = \sqrt{-1}$, $i^2 = -1$:

$$(5 - 2i)(5 + 2i) = 25 - 4i^2 = 25 - 4(-1) = 25 + 4 = 29$$

Adding and Subtracting Complex Numbers

These operations use a concept you are already familiar with: combining like terms. When performing subtraction, remember to distribute the negative.

Example

Solve $(2 - 4i) - (5 + i)$.

$$(2 - 4i) - (5 + i) = -3 - 5i$$

Multiplying and Dividing Complex Numbers

In the discussion of the complex conjugate, you saw how to multiply two complex numbers (apply FOIL and then combine like terms where necessary). Now let's talk about dividing complex numbers.

Remember that division can be presented as a regular division problem or a fraction. For example, $\frac{1}{2} = 1 \div 2$. Often, division problems with complex numbers will be written as fractions. To divide two complex numbers, multiply by the conjugate of the denominator.

Example

Simplify $\dfrac{3-5i}{4+i}$.

$$\frac{3-5i}{4+i} = \frac{3-5i}{4+i}\left(\frac{4-i}{4-i}\right) = \frac{12-23i+5i^2}{16-i^2} = \frac{12-23i-5}{16+1} = \frac{7-23i}{17}$$

Powers of *i*

You know that $i^2 = -1$, but what about other powers of *i*? These powers follow a cyclical pattern.

Powers of *i*
$i^1 = i$
$i^2 = -1$
$i^3 = -i$
$i^4 = 1$

This pattern repeats as you go into higher powers. For example, $i^5 = \sqrt{-1}$ or *i*, and $i^{24} = 1$.

When simplifying a power of *i*, always use the pattern. Write the exponents using rules of exponents in terms of one of these four powers.

Example

Find i^{52}.

$$i^{52} = i^{4\cdot3} = (i^4)^{13} = (1)^{13} = 1$$

EQUATIONS AND INEQUALITIES

In this section, you'll review solving different types of equations and inequalities. These questions form a key area of algebra study, representing 44% of all questions on the test.

Linear Equations and Inequalities

Linear equations and inequalities have a variable but no exponent. Solve these by "undoing" operations to isolate the variable. If something is being added, you subtract and vice versa. If something is multiplied, you divide (or multiply by a fraction). Remember that whatever you do to one side of the equation or inequality, you must also do to the other. Here's a simple example.

Example

Solve the equation: $3x + 3 = 18$

First, isolate the variable on the left side. What you do to one side, you must also do to the other.

$$3x + 3 - 3 = 18 - 3$$
$$3x = 15$$

Next, eliminate the coefficient on the variable by performing the inverse operation, division in this case.

$$3x \div 3 = 15 \div 3$$
$$x = 5$$

And that's it. Here's a more complex example:

Example

Solve the equation: $\dfrac{1}{2}x + \dfrac{2}{3} = \dfrac{3}{4}(x - 1)$

As a first step, distribute the fraction on the right-hand side:

$$\frac{1}{2}x + \frac{2}{3} = \frac{3}{4}x - \frac{3}{4}$$

Now there are x terms on both sides of the equation. Move your x's to one side and then combine like terms to isolate the x variable:

$$\frac{1}{2}x - \frac{3}{4}x + \frac{2}{3} = \frac{3}{4}x - \frac{3}{4} - \frac{3}{4}$$
$$-\frac{1}{4}x + \frac{2}{3} = -\frac{3}{4}$$

Now subtract $\dfrac{2}{3}$ from both sides to isolate the x term:

$$-\frac{1}{4}x + \frac{2}{3} - \frac{2}{3} = -\frac{3}{4} - \frac{2}{3}$$
$$-\frac{1}{4}x = -\frac{17}{12}$$

The last step is to multiply both sides by -4:

$$-4\left(-\frac{1}{4}x\right) = -4\left(-\frac{17}{12}\right)$$

$$x = \frac{68}{12} = \frac{17}{3}$$

Inequalities are solved in the same way. However, there is a special rule: anytime you multiply or divide by a negative, flip the direction of the inequality.

Example

Solve $3x - 5 > 10x$.

$$3x - 5 > 10x$$

$$-7x > 5$$

$$x < -\frac{5}{7}$$

The solutions to inequalities can also be graphed or written in interval notation.

Typical Intervals			
$a \leq x \leq b$	$[a, b]$	both a and b are included	
$a \leq x < b$	$[a, b)$	a is included but b is not	
$a < x \leq b$	$(a, b]$	b is included but a is not	
$a < x < b$	(a, b)	neither a nor b are included	
$x < a$	$(-\infty, a)$	a is not included	
$x \leq a$	$(-\infty, a]$	a is included	
$x < a$ and $x > b$	$(-\infty, a) \cup (b, \infty)$	neither a nor b are included*	

* If a or b were included, then the "[" symbol would be used in place of the "(".
Therefore, the solution to the inequality above could be written as $\left(-\infty, -\frac{5}{7}\right)$.

Quadratic Equations and Inequalities

Solving by Factoring

A quadratic equation has the form $ax^2 + bx + c = 0$, where $a \neq 0$. Quadratic equations can be solved using the standard method of factoring. This method requires you to think about the reverse FOILing method discussed in the Factoring Polynomials section.

Example

Solve the equation $2x^2 + 11x + 5 = 0$.

Factor the quadratic into the form $(ax + b)(cx + d)$. In this case, the following must be true: $ac = 2$, $bd = 5$, and $ad + bc = 11$. For ac, the factors of 2 are 1 and 2. For bd, the factors of 5 are 1 and 5. Try the values and see if they work:

$$2x^2 + 11x + 5 = 0$$
$$(2x + 1)(x + 5) = 0$$

Sure enough, they do. Next, solve for $2x + 1 = 0$ or $x + 5 = 0$. When we solve both equations, we find that $x = -\dfrac{1}{2}$ and $x = -5$.

Example

Solve the equation $x^2 = 7$.

We can solve this problem by using a factoring rule:

$$x^2 = 7$$
$$x^2 - 7 = 0$$
$$(x - \sqrt{7})(x + \sqrt{7}) = 0$$

Next, solve the equations $(x - \sqrt{7}) = 0$ and $(x + \sqrt{7}) = 0$. We find that $x = +\sqrt{7}$ and $x = -\sqrt{7}$. We express these solutions as $x = -\sqrt{7}$.

The Quadratic Formula

For the most difficult quadratic equations, the quadratic formula is the best method for finding solutions. You can solve any quadratic equation using the following method.

If $ax^2 + bx + c = 0$, where $a \neq 0$, then the roots of the equation are given by the following:

$$x = \frac{-b - \sqrt{b^2 - 4ac}}{2a}$$

Example

Solve: $x^2 + 2x - 6 = 0$

Let $a = 1$, $b = 2$, and $c = -6$ and solve:

$$x = \frac{-(2) - \sqrt{(2)^2 - 4(1)(-6)}}{2(1)}$$

$$x = \frac{-(2) - \sqrt{4 + 24}}{2}$$

$$x = \frac{-(2) - \sqrt{28}}{2}$$

$$x = \frac{-2 - \sqrt{(4)(7)}}{2}$$

$$x = \frac{-2 - 2\sqrt{7}}{2}$$

$$x = -1 - \sqrt{7}$$

Quadratic Inequalities

Working with quadratic inequalities requires not only comfort with the rules for quadratic equations but also familiarity with an additional set of rules apart from what you encounter with linear equations and inequalities.

Follow these steps to solve quadratic inequalities:

- Step 1: Rewrite the inequality so that one side equals zero and factor the quadratic.
- Step 2: Solve the corresponding equation.
- Step 3: Draw a number line and label the solutions.
- Step 4: Test each possible solution "region" using a value from that region in the quadratic (a number before the lowest solution, between the two solutions, and after the greatest solution).

The following example demonstrates these steps.

Example

Find the solution to $x^2 + 2x > 3$.

Use the steps for solving quadratic inequalities:

Step 1: Rewrite the inequality so that one side equals zero and factor the quadratic:

$$x^2 + 2x > 3$$
$$x^2 + 2x - 3 > 0$$
$$x^2 + 2x - 3 = 0$$
$$(x + 3)(x - 1) = 0$$

Step 2: Solve the corresponding equation (i.e., find solutions for $x^2 + 2x - 3 = 0$):

$$(x + 3)(x - 1) = 0$$
$$x + 3 = 0 \text{ and } x - 1 = 0$$

Thus $x = -3$ and 1, so any regions that make the inequality true will have strict boundaries at -3 and 1.

Step 3: Plot the values for x on a number line:

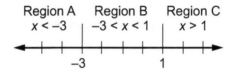

Step 4: Test each region with a value from that region and determine if the original inequality is true or false.

Pick any value from each region and test the value in the original inequality written in terms of zero ($x^2 + 2x - 3 > 0$) and determine if the solution is positive or negative. Any value that satisfies the original inequality is part of the solution set.

Region A: Test value $x = -4$:

$$(-4)^2 + 2(-4) - 3 = 16 - 8 - 3$$
$$= 5 \text{ positive}$$

Region B: Test value $x = 0$ or $(0)^2 + 2(0) - 3 = -3$ negative

Region C: Test value $x = 2$ or $(2)^2 + 2(2) - 3 = 5$ positive

So, we find that the solution is positive for region A and C, where $x < -3$ and $x > 1$ or $\left(-\infty, -3\right) \cup \left(1, \infty\right)$.

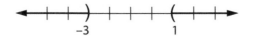

Absolute Value Equations and Inequalities

The distance of any number from zero along the real number line is the **absolute value**. Pipes "| |" are used around a value to indicate absolute value. For example, $|4| = 4$ and $|-4| = 4$. Absolute value graphs are in a V shape, as shown by the following:

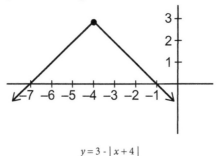

$$y = 3 - |x + 4|$$

To solve an absolute value equation, set up two equations, one for each possible sign. Before you do this, though, the absolute value must be isolated.

Example

Solve: $|5x + 1| - 3 = 0$.

Isolate the absolute value.

$$|5x + 1| = 3$$

Write two equations, one with 3 and one with –3. Solve each equation to get the solutions to the absolute value:

$$
\begin{array}{ll}
5x + 1 = 3 & 5x + 1 = -3 \\
5x = 2 & 5x = -4 \\
x = \dfrac{5}{2} & x = -\dfrac{4}{5}
\end{array}
$$

The two solutions are $x = \dfrac{5}{2}$ and $x = -\dfrac{4}{5}$.

The rules for solving absolute value inequalities are shown here. The same rules apply if you have $\leq$ or $\geq$ signs.

Rules for Solving Absolute Value Inequalities

Given	Solve
$\lvert a \rvert < b$	$-b < a < b$
$\lvert a \rvert > b$	$a < -b$ or $a > b$

Example

Solve $\frac{1}{2}\lvert 2x - 4 \rvert < 5$.

Isolate the absolute value:

$$\frac{1}{2}\lvert 2x - 4 \rvert < 5$$
$$\lvert 2x - 4 \rvert < 10$$

Now apply the rules from the table:

$$-10 < 2x - 4 < 10$$
$$-6 < 2x < 14$$
$$-3 < x < 7$$

Systems of Linear Equations and Inequalities

A system of linear equations or inequalities is a group of linear equations or inequalities where all statements must be true at the same time. These are each approached using different methods, represented in the following section.

Systems of linear equations can be solved using two methods: elimination and substitution. However, elimination is often the easiest approach and works for all systems of equations you may come across.

The Elimination Method

Elimination is based upon the principle that an equation is equivalent if a value is multiplied, divided, added, or subtracted on both sides of an equation. Note that for multiplication and division, the number must be non-zero.

Using this method, simultaneous equations can be transformed so that when the equations are added or subtracted, variables are eliminated, thus allowing the equations to be solved. This method can take fewer steps than the substitution method, but it requires that the proper transformations be used.

Example

Using the elimination method, find the solutions of the system:

$$x + 3y = -1$$
$$2x - y = 5$$

First, we can multiply equation 1 by -2. The value -2 is selected to allow us to eliminate the $2x$ by addition. After multiplying, add equation 2 to equation 1:

$$
\begin{aligned}
-2x - 6y &= 2 \\
+ \quad 2x - y &= 5 \\
\hline
-7y &= 7
\end{aligned}
$$

Now we can easily solve, and we find $y = -1$. We can then substitute this value into either equation and obtain the value of $x = 2$.

Systems of linear *inequalities* are solved graphically. All points within a shaded region are solutions and all points outside of a shaded region are not solutions. You can review how to graph linear equations in the section on polynomials and their graphs.

Before we look at solving a system of inequalities, let's note that you can check whether you have a solution or not by testing it in each inequality. For example, take the system $\dfrac{3x + y < 5}{2x - 9y < 4}$. The point (10, 10) is a solution.

You can check this by substituting 10 into x and y and see that you have two true statements. Therefore, the inequalities must both be true.

Example

Graph the solution set to the system of inequalities: $\begin{aligned} 3x + y &< 5 \\ 2x - 9y &< 4 \end{aligned}$.

First, write each inequality in terms of y. Remember to flip the direction of the inequality when you divide or multiply by a negative:

$$y < -3x + 5$$

$$y > \frac{2}{9}x - \frac{4}{9}$$

Now graph each inequality as though it were an equation. Shade the region above the line if it is >, shade the region below the line if it is <. Use a solid line if you have a less than or equal to or a greater than or equal to sign ($\leq$ or $\geq$). Use a dotted line when graphing inequalities with < or >.

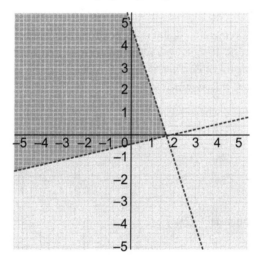

The region where the two shaded regions overlap is the solution set. Any point from this region is a solution to the inequality.

Exponential and Logarithmic Equations

Exponential and logarithmic equations are related to each other by the fact that the exponential is the inverse of the logarithm and vice-versa. We use this fact to solve the equations.

Exponential Equations

In an exponential equation, the variable is an exponent. For example, $4^x = 1$ and $3e^x - 1 = 2$. To solve exponential equations, express each side of the equation as a power of the same base. If the bases are the same, then the exponents can be said to be equal. For example, $2^x = 16$ becomes $2^x = 2^4$, thus $x = 4$.

Additionally, you can use logarithms. Logarithms express the relationship that $y = \log_b a \Leftrightarrow b^y = a$. For the previous example, how many 2s do you need to multiply together to get 16? If you write this in exponential and logarithmic forms, you have $2^x = 16 \Leftrightarrow x = \log_2 16$. You need $2 \times 2 \times 2 \times 2$ or four 2s. Thus, you have $2^4 = 16 \Leftrightarrow 4 = \log_2 16$. When both sides of an exponential equation do not share a common base, however, you will take the log of both sides instead.

When you see e, remember that it is a special constant with an approximate value of 2.7182818. Its corresponding logarithm is called the natural log and is written as $\ln(x)$. Further, if there is no base on the log (the b in the earlier equations), it is assumed to be 10.

Here's an example where both sides of the exponential equation lack a common base.

Example

Solve $4(3^{3x}) = 5$.

Isolate the exponential term:

$$4(3^{3x}) = 5$$

$$3^{3x} = \frac{5}{4}$$

Take log base 3 of both sides and solve:

$$\log_3(3^{3x}) = \log_3\left(\frac{5}{4}\right)$$

$$3x = \log_3\left(\frac{5}{4}\right)$$

$$x = \frac{1}{3}\log_3\left(\frac{5}{4}\right)$$

The solution is typically left in this form.

Logarithmic Equations

To solve logarithmic equations, use the same concept except take each side to the power of the base of the logarithm. When working with logarithms, you may find the following rules helpful:

Log Rules

$$\log_b(MN) = \log_b M + \log_b N$$

$$\log_b\left(\frac{M}{N}\right) = \log_b M - \log_b N$$

$$\log_b(M^p) = p\log_b(M)$$

Example

Solve: $\log(-3x) - \log(2x + 4) = 1$

Use the log rules to isolate the log term. Then take both sides to the 10th power since this is assumed to be base 10:

$$\log(-3x) - \log(2x + 4) = 1$$

$$\log\left(\frac{-3x}{2x + 4}\right) = 1$$

$$10^{\log\left(\frac{-3x}{2x+4}\right)} = 10^1$$

$$\frac{-3x}{2x + 4} = 10$$

$$10(2x + 4) = -3x$$

$$20x + 40 = -3x$$

$$23x = -40$$

$$x = \frac{-40}{23} = -\frac{40}{23}$$

Let's look at an example with the natural log.

Example

Simplify: $\ln\left(\dfrac{10}{x^e}\right)$

Use the log rules for division to rewrite the log. The exponent on the second natural log then becomes a coefficient for the term:

$$\ln\left(\frac{10}{x^e}\right) = \ln 10 - \ln x^e$$
$$= \ln 10 - e \ln x$$

Equations Involving Radicals

Solving equations with radicals involves a few simple steps. The Fractional Exponents section introduced radical expressions laws:

$$\sqrt[n]{a} = a^{\frac{1}{n}}$$
$$a^{\frac{m}{n}} = \sqrt[n]{a^m}$$
$$\sqrt[n]{a} \cdot \sqrt[n]{b} = \sqrt[n]{ab}$$
$$\sqrt[n]{\frac{a}{b}} = \frac{\sqrt[n]{a}}{\sqrt[n]{b}}$$
$$\sqrt[nm]{a} = \sqrt[m]{\sqrt[n]{a}}$$
$$\sqrt[n]{a^n} = a$$

Use those rules along with the following steps:

- Step 1: Move one radical to one side of the equation and everything else to the other side.
- Step 2: Eliminate the radical by raising both sides by a power that is the reciprocal of the exponent.
- Step 3: Repeat steps 1 and 2 if radicals are still present.
- Step 4: Solve the remaining equation.
- Step 5: Check for extraneous solutions (received values that are not actual solutions).

Example

Solve the radical equation $\sqrt{10x - 4} - 4 = 0$.

Step 1: Isolate the radical by putting it on one side:

$$\sqrt{10x - 4} = 4$$

Step 2: Get rid of the radical by squaring both sides of the equation:

$$\left(\sqrt{10x - 4}\right)^2 = 4^2$$
$$10x - 4 = 16$$

Step 3: All radicals are eliminated, so proceed to step 4.

Step 4: Solve the remaining equation:

$$10x - 4 = 16$$
$$10x = 20$$
$$x = 2$$

Step 5: Check the solution:

$$\sqrt{10(2) - 4} - 4 = 0$$
$$\sqrt{16} - 4 = 0$$
$$0 = 0$$

The solution is $x = 2$.

Rational exponents, which are of the form $a^{\frac{m}{n}} = b$, are solved using the same steps as above. If needed, read about the rules for exponents in the Operations with Positive, Negative, and Fractional Exponents section for more instruction.

Example

Solve the rational equation $\left(x^2 + x - 5\right)^{\frac{2}{3}} - 1 = 0$.

Step 1: Isolate the rational exponent by putting it on one side:

$$\left(x^2 + x - 5\right)^{\frac{2}{3}} = 1$$

Step 2: Get rid of the rational exponent by raising to the inverse of the exponent, or $\frac{3}{2}$:

$$\left(x^2 + x - 5\right)^{\frac{2}{3}} = (1)^{\frac{3}{2}}$$
$$x^2 + x - 5 = 1$$

Note: $(1)^{\frac{3}{2}} = \sqrt[2]{(1)^3} = \sqrt[2]{1} = 1$.

Step 3: All radicals are eliminated, so proceed to step 4.

Step 4: Solve the remaining equation:

$$x^2 + x - 5 = 1$$
$$x^2 + x - 6 = 0$$
$$(x + 3)(x - 2) = 0$$

Thus, $x = -3$ and $x = 2$ are two possible solutions.

Step 5: Check the solution for -3:

$$\left((-3)^2 + (-3) - 5\right)^{\frac{2}{3}} - 1 = 0$$
$$(9 - 3 - 5)^{\frac{2}{3}} - 1 = 0$$
$$1^{\frac{2}{3}} - 1 = 0$$
$$0 = 0$$

We have shown that -3 is a valid solution. Now check $x = 2$.

$$\left((2)^2 + 2 - 5\right)^{\frac{2}{3}} - 1 = 0$$
$$(4 + 2 - 5)^{\frac{2}{3}} - 1 = 0$$
$$(1)^{\frac{2}{3}} - 1 = 0$$
$$1 - 1 = 0$$

So, both 2 and -3 are roots to $\left(x^2 + x - 5\right)^{\frac{2}{3}} - 1 = 0$.

PROPERTIES OF FUNCTIONS AND THEIR GRAPHS

Functions are rules that give one value y for a single input x. The notation for a function of x is $f(x)$. You can evaluate functions by plugging in an x value and finding the corresponding output.

Example

Evaluate the function $f(x) = 2^x - 14$ for $x = 4$.

Replace each x with 4. The notation for this is $f(4)$:

$$f(4) = 2^4 - 14 = 16 - 14 = 2$$

Coordinate Systems

The values of a function $y = f(x)$ can be plotted in the xy-coordinate plane, sometimes called a Cartesian coordinate system. In this plane, inputs x are represented by the horizontal axis and outputs y are represented by the vertical axis. Different parts of this plane are called quadrants.

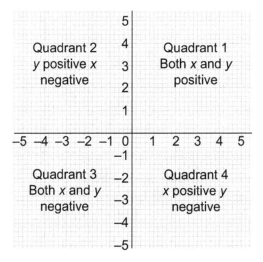

In the previous example, the input is 4 and the output is 2. This is represented by the point (4, 2) and would be in Quadrant 1.

For any function, there may be a point where it crosses the x-axis or the y-axis. These points are known as the y-intercept and x-intercept. You find the x-intercept(s) by setting y equal to 0 and solving. Similarly, find the y-intercept by setting x equal to 0 and solving.

Domain and Range

The **domain** of a function is all real x values for which the function is defined. The **range** of a function is all real y values for which the function is defined. Remember, when considering the domain, you can't divide by 0 or take the square root of a negative number, which would result in an imaginary number. Since there is no division or roots in a polynomial, the domain of any polynomial function is all real numbers or $(-\infty, \infty)$.

Example

Find the domain of $f(x) = \sqrt{2x - 1}$

Since you can't take the square root of a negative number, the domain is all values where the expression under the radical is positive or zero.

$$2x - 1 \geq 0$$
$$2x \geq 1$$
$$x \geq \frac{1}{2}$$

So, the domain is all real numbers where $x \geq \frac{1}{2}$, or $\left[\frac{1}{2}, \infty\right)$.

Example

Find the range of the function $f(x) = 3(x - 2)^2 - 7$.

This is a quadratic function, the graph of which creates a parabola. This quadratic is in vertex form, $y = a(x - h)^2 + k$, which allows you to find the vertex (h, k) quickly. For this function, the vertex is $(2, -7)$. That means that one of the boundaries for the range will be the y value -7. To determine whether the range contains y values toward ∞ or $-\infty$, you need to look at the a value of the equation. If it is negative, the parabola will open downward, but since a is positive, this graph opens upward. Thus, the range for the function is $f(x) \geq -7$, or $[-7, \infty)$.

Operations of Functions

Functions can be added, subtracted, multiplied, and divided. Function operations work just like operations on expressions (found in the Fundamental Algebra Operations section). The notation for these operations is in the following table:

Function Operations

Sum of f and g	$(f+g)(x) = f(x) + g(x)$
Difference of f and g	$(f-g)(x) = f(x) - g(x)$
Product of f and g	$(f \bullet g)(x) = f(x) \times g(x)$
Quotient of f and g	$\left(\dfrac{f}{g}\right)(x) = \dfrac{f(x)}{g(x)}$
Composite function	$(f \bullet g)(x) = f(g(x))$

The new operation here is function composition. This operation allows you to find the function of another function. The input is now a function instead of a value for x.

Example

Find $(f \circ g)(x)$ for $f(x) = 2x - x^2$ and $g(x) = x + 1$.

Replace each x in $f(x)$ with $x + 1$. Then, simplify:

$$
\begin{aligned}
(f \circ g)(x) = f(g(x)) &= 2(g(x)) - (g(x))^2 \\
&= 2(x+1) - (x+1)^2 \\
&= 2x + 2 - (x^2 + 2x + 1) \\
&= 2x + 2 - x^2 - 2x - 1 \\
&= -x^2 + 1
\end{aligned}
$$

Inverse Functions

Inverse functions are based on a given function $f(x)$. The notation of an inverse to f is $f^{-1}(x)$. These functions "undo" each other. That is $f(f^{-1}(x)) = f^{-1}(f(x)) = x$. The graphs of the two functions are the same but are reflected across the line $y = x$.

To find the inverse of a function, let $y = f(x)$, switch x and y values and then solve for y.

Example

Find $f^{-1}(x)$ for the function $f(x) = 5x - 7$.

$$y = 5x - 7$$
$$x = 5y - 7$$
$$x + 7 = 5y$$
$$y = \frac{x + 7}{5}$$

Thus $f^{-1}(x) = \frac{x + 7}{5}$.

Linear Functions

Linear functions are functions of the form $y = f(x) = mx + b$. When graphed as a line, it will have a slope (steepness) m and y-intercept (where it crosses the y-axis) of b.

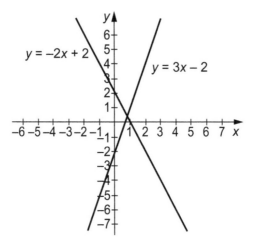

Example of Two Different Lines, $f(x) = -2x + 2$ and $f(x) = 3x - 2$

Finding Slope

Slope is the steepness of a line. Think of slope as a fraction in which the numerator indicates the vertical change from one point to another on the line (moving left to right) corresponding to a given horizontal change, indicated by the fraction's denominator. As such, slope is often called **rise over run**. Lines with positive slope rise from left to right, and lines with negative slope fall from left to right. The slope of a line passing through the points (x_1, y_1) and (x_2, y_2) can be found using the formula: $m = \dfrac{y_2 - y_1}{x_2 - x_1}$.

Example

Find the slope of a line passing through the points (2, 6) and (−1, 4).

$$m = \frac{y_2 - y_1}{x_2 - x_1} = \frac{4-6}{-1-2} = \frac{-2}{-3} = \frac{2}{3}$$

The slope of the line is $\frac{2}{3}$. For every 2 units the line rises on the y-axis, the line will run 3 units to the right on the x-axis.

Finding the Equation of a Line

The equation of any line can be found using the formula $y - y_1 = m(x - x_1)$. If you are given two points, you will have to find the slope first.

Example

Find the equation of a line passing through (3, 1) with slope $\frac{1}{2}$.

Apply the formula and solve for y:

$$y - y_1 = m(x - x_1)$$
$$y - 1 = \frac{1}{2}(x - 3)$$
$$y = \frac{1}{2}x - \frac{3}{2} + 1$$
$$y = \frac{1}{2}x - \frac{1}{2}$$

Quadratic Functions

A **quadratic function** is any function of the form $f(x) = ax^2 + bx + c$ where a, b, and c are real numbers. The shape of the graph of a quadratic function is called a **parabola**. It reaches a maximum or minimum height called the **vertex**.

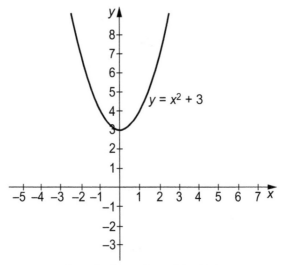

Example of a Quadratic, $f(x) = x^2 + 3$

When $a > 0$, the graph opens up. When $a < 0$, the graph opens down. The x-coordinate of the vertex can be found using the formula $-\dfrac{b}{2a}$. The resulting value can then be substituted into the function to find the y-coordinate.

Example

Find the minimum value reached by the function $f(x) = x^2 - 6x + 1$.

The minimum value is reached when $x = -\dfrac{b}{2a} = -\dfrac{-6}{2} = 3$. Evaluate the function for 3 to find the minimum value:

$$f(3) = 3^2 - 6(3) + 1 = 9 - 18 + 1 = -8$$

Thus, the vertex is at $(3, -8)$, and the minimum value reached by the function is -8.

Polynomial Functions

Polynomial functions have the same form as polynomial expressions. Polynomial functions have variables taken to a power, are multiplied by some coefficient, and then are added together. For example, $f(x) = -x^3 + 4x^2 - x$. Technically, both linear functions and quadratic functions are polynomial functions. But they have special properties, as shown in the previous sections. We will focus on polynomials where the **degree** (highest power) is 3 or greater.

The graphs of polynomial functions are curves with turning points where they change direction.

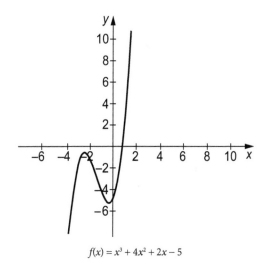

$$f(x) = x^3 + 4x^2 + 2x - 5$$

The number of turning points is equal to the degree minus 1. The polynomial function shown in the figure has a degree of 3 and two turning points.

The end behavior of a polynomial function can be determined by the degree of the polynomial and the coefficient of the highest degree term. The table below explains these properties.

Degree	Sign of the Highest Degree Term	End Behavior
Even	Positive	Rises on both left and right
Even	Negative	Falls on both left and right
Odd	Positive	Falls on left, rises on right
Odd	Negative	Rises on left, falls on right

Rational Functions

Rational functions are similar to rational expressions. Their domain is determined by the denominator. When the denominator is zero, the value is not included in the domain. Further, rational functions have **asymptotes**. The function approaches these lines but never crosses them.

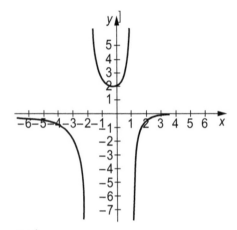

Graph of $f(x) = \dfrac{x-4}{x^2+x-2}$, with two vertical asymptotes and one horizontal asymptote

To find the vertical asymptotes of a rational function, find all values where the denominator is 0 but the numerator is not 0.

Example

Find all vertical asymptotes of the function $f(x) = \dfrac{x^2 - x - 2}{x^2 - 2x - 3}$.

$$f(x) = \frac{x^2 - x - 2}{x^2 - 2x - 3} = \frac{(x+1)(x-2)}{(x+1)(x-3)}$$

The denominator is 0 whenever $x = -1$ or 3. However, -1 also makes the numerator 0, so the only vertical asymptote is $x = 3$.

Horizontal asymptotes are found by looking at the degrees of the highest degree terms. The following table shows the rules for this.

Degrees of the terms	Horizontal asymptote
The same	$y =$ the ratio of the coefficients. Ex: $y = \dfrac{2x^3 - 4}{5x^3}$ has horizontal asymptote $y = \dfrac{2}{5}$.
Higher degree in the numerator	No horizontal asymptote
Lower degree in numerator	$y = 0$ is the horizontal asymptote

The function in the example has a horizontal asymptote of $y = 1$ since the degrees are the same and the coefficients are both 1.

Exponential and Logarithmic Functions

Exponential functions are functions where the exponent is a variable. Logarithmic functions include a log of some base as part of their definition.

Exponential Functions

The graph of an exponential function $f(x) = b^x$ has a horizonal asymptote of the x-axis—that is $y = 0$. If the base is a whole number, the graph rises rapidly on the right. If the base is a fraction or decimal, the graph falls quickly from left to right.

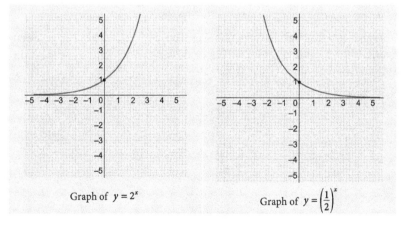

Graph of $y = 2^x$ Graph of $y = \left(\dfrac{1}{2}\right)^x$

Logarithmic Functions

Logarithmic functions are inverse functions to exponential functions. Their graphs are a reflection across $y = x$ of the graph of the corresponding exponential function. The graph of a logarithmic function $f(x) = \log_b(x)$ has a vertical asymptote of the y-axis—that is $x = 0$. The graph rises from left to right, but not as quickly as an exponential function.

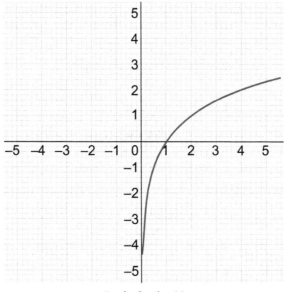

Graph of $y = \log_2(x)$

Note that if a function like the one seen above is translated, that is rewritten by adding or subtracting within or outside the function, the locations of the asymptotes may change.

SUMMING IT UP

- When working with algebraic expressions, you can only combine like terms. Like terms have the same variable and exponent: x^2 and $-2x^2$ are like terms; $2x^4$ and $2x^5$ are not.
- When subtracting polynomials, always remember to distribute the negative to every term in parentheses of the second polynomial.
- When multiplying two monomials, multiply coefficients and add exponents.
- When multiplying two binomials, use the FOIL method (first, outer, inner, last).
- When multiplying binomials and trinomials together, every term in the second polynomial must be multiplied by every term in the first polynomial.
- Factoring polynomials identifies the polynomials that were multiplied together. Here are some factorizations to memorize:

$$x^2 - y^2 = (x + y)(x - y)$$
$$x^2 + 2xy + y^2 = (x + y)^2$$
$$x^2 - 2xy + y^2 = (x - y)^2$$
$$x^3 + 3x^2y + 3xy^2 + y^3 = (x + y)^3$$
$$x^3 - 3x^2y + 3xy^2 - y^3 = (x - y)^3$$

- When factoring polynomials of the form $ax^2 + bx + c$, use the FOIL method in reverse or factor out common factors of all the terms in the polynomial.
- To simplify a rational expression, cancel common factors shared by both the numerator and the denominator of the expression.
- To add and subtract rational expressions, find a common denominator. Don't forget to distribute the negative when subtracting.
- Multiply rational expressions straight across. You do not need a common denominator. You can cross-cancel, finding common factors to eliminate from both the numerator and denominator.
- Divide rational expressions by "flipping" the second fraction, then multiplying. You can then cross-cancel.

- Remember the following rules for exponents:

Product	$a^m a^n = a^{m+n}$
Product of a power	$(a^m)^n = a^{mn}$
Quotient to a power	$\left(\dfrac{a}{b}\right)^n = \dfrac{a^n}{b^n}$
Quotient	$\dfrac{a^m}{a^n} = a^{m-n}$
Zero exponent	$a^0 = 1$
Negative exponent	$a^{-n} = \dfrac{1}{a^n}$
Inversion	$\left(\dfrac{a}{b}\right)^{-n} = \left(\dfrac{b}{a}\right)^n$
Fractional powers	$a^{\frac{m}{n}} = \sqrt[n]{a^m}$

- Know the following laws for radical expressions:

$$\sqrt[n]{a} = a^{\frac{1}{n}}$$

$$a^{\frac{m}{n}} = \sqrt[n]{a^m}$$

$$\sqrt[n]{a} \cdot \sqrt[n]{b} = \sqrt[n]{ab}$$

$$\sqrt[n]{\frac{a}{b}} = \frac{\sqrt[n]{a}}{\sqrt[n]{b}}$$

$$\sqrt[nm]{a} = \sqrt[m]{\sqrt[n]{a}}$$

$$\sqrt[n]{a^n} = a$$

- Complex numbers are numbers of the form $a + bi$, where a and b are real numbers and $i = \sqrt{-1}$. The conjugate of a complex number $a + bi$ is $a - bi$.
- To divide two complex numbers, multiply by the conjugate of the denominator.
- Memorize the powers of i:

$$i^1 = i$$

$$i^2 = -1$$

$$i^3 = -i$$

$$i^4 = 1$$

- When solving inequalities, you must flip the direction of the inequality any time you multiply or divide by a negative.
- Solve quadratic equations ($ax^2 + bx + c = 0$) by using FOIL in reverse.
- If $a \neq 0$ in $ax^2 + bx + c = 0$, then the roots of the equation are given by the quadratic equation:

$$x = \frac{-b - \sqrt{b^2 - 4ac}}{2a}$$

- To solve quadratic inequalities
  - Step 1: Rewrite the inequality so that one side equals zero and factor the quadratic.
  - Step 2: Solve the corresponding equation.
  - Step 3: Draw a number line and label the solutions.
  - Step 4: Test each possible solution "region" using a value from that region in the quadratic.
- To solve an absolute value equation, set up an equation for each possible sign. You must first isolate the variable.
- You can solve a system of linear equations by elimination or substitution; when in doubt, use elimination, as it works for all systems of equations you may come across.
- When solving linear inequalities graphically, all points within the shaded region are solutions, and all points outside of a shaded region are not solutions.
- To solve exponential equations, use the relationship $y = \log_b a \Leftrightarrow b^y = a$.
- The term e is a special constant and its corresponding logarithm, $\ln(x)$, is called the natural log.
- Remember the following log rules:

$$\log_b(MN) = \log_b M + \log_b N$$
$$\log_b\left(\frac{M}{N}\right) = \log_b M - \log_b N$$
$$\log_b(M^p) = p\log_b(M)$$

- To solve equations with radicals
  - Step 1: Move one radical to one side.
  - Step 2: Eliminate the radical.
  - Step 3: Repeat steps 1 and 2 until all radicals are gone.
  - Step 4: Solve the remaining equation.
  - Step 5: Check for extraneous solutions.
- Evaluate functions by plugging in an x value and finding the corresponding output.

- In quadrant 1, both x and y are positive; in quadrant 2, y is positive and x is negative; in quadrant 3, both x and y are negative; in quadrant 4, x is positive and y is negative.
- The domain of a function is the set of real x values for which the function is defined, and for any polynomial function, the domain is all real numbers: $(-\infty, \infty)$. The range of a function is the set of real y values for which the function is defined.
- To find the inverse of a function, let $y = f(x)$, switch x and y values and then solve for y.
- The form of linear functions is $y = f(x) = mx + b$; this represents a line with slope m and a y-intercept of b.
- The slope of a line passing through the points (x_1, y_1) and (x_2, y_2) can be found using the formula: $m = \dfrac{y_2 - y_1}{x_2 - x_1}$.
- The equation of any line can be found using the formula $y - y_1 = m(x - x_1)$.
- The x-coordinate of the vertex of a parabola, found from a quadratic function, can be found using the formula $-\dfrac{b}{2a}$.
- Determine the end behavior of a polynomial function by the degree of the polynomial and the coefficient of the highest degree term:

Degree	Sign of the Highest Degree Term	End Behavior
Even	Positive	Rises on both left and right
Even	Negative	Falls on both left and right
Odd	Positive	Falls on left, rises on right
Odd	Negative	Rises on left, falls on right

- To find the vertical asymptotes of a rational function, find all values where the denominator is 0 but the numerator is not 0.
  - The graph of an exponential function $f(x) = b^x$ has a horizonal asymptote when $y = 0$.
  - The graph of a logarithmic function $f(x) = \log_b(x)$ has a vertical asymptote when $x = 0$.

Chapter 4

Fundamentals of College Algebra Post-Test

POST-TEST ANSWER SHEET

1. Ⓐ Ⓑ Ⓒ Ⓓ
2. Ⓐ Ⓑ Ⓒ Ⓓ
3. Ⓐ Ⓑ Ⓒ Ⓓ
4. Ⓐ Ⓑ Ⓒ Ⓓ
5. Ⓐ Ⓑ Ⓒ Ⓓ
6. Ⓐ Ⓑ Ⓒ Ⓓ
7. Ⓐ Ⓑ Ⓒ Ⓓ
8. Ⓐ Ⓑ Ⓒ Ⓓ
9. Ⓐ Ⓑ Ⓒ Ⓓ
10. Ⓐ Ⓑ Ⓒ Ⓓ
11. Ⓐ Ⓑ Ⓒ Ⓓ
12. Ⓐ Ⓑ Ⓒ Ⓓ
13. Ⓐ Ⓑ Ⓒ Ⓓ
14. Ⓐ Ⓑ Ⓒ Ⓓ
15. Ⓐ Ⓑ Ⓒ Ⓓ

16. Ⓐ Ⓑ Ⓒ Ⓓ
17. Ⓐ Ⓑ Ⓒ Ⓓ
18. Ⓐ Ⓑ Ⓒ Ⓓ
19. Ⓐ Ⓑ Ⓒ Ⓓ
20. Ⓐ Ⓑ Ⓒ Ⓓ
21. Ⓐ Ⓑ Ⓒ Ⓓ
22. Ⓐ Ⓑ Ⓒ Ⓓ
23. Ⓐ Ⓑ Ⓒ Ⓓ
24. Ⓐ Ⓑ Ⓒ Ⓓ
25. Ⓐ Ⓑ Ⓒ Ⓓ
26. Ⓐ Ⓑ Ⓒ Ⓓ
27. Ⓐ Ⓑ Ⓒ Ⓓ
28. Ⓐ Ⓑ Ⓒ Ⓓ
29. Ⓐ Ⓑ Ⓒ Ⓓ
30. Ⓐ Ⓑ Ⓒ Ⓓ

31. Ⓐ Ⓑ Ⓒ Ⓓ
32. Ⓐ Ⓑ Ⓒ Ⓓ
33. Ⓐ Ⓑ Ⓒ Ⓓ
34. Ⓐ Ⓑ Ⓒ Ⓓ
35. Ⓐ Ⓑ Ⓒ Ⓓ
36. Ⓐ Ⓑ Ⓒ Ⓓ
37. Ⓐ Ⓑ Ⓒ Ⓓ
38. Ⓐ Ⓑ Ⓒ Ⓓ
39. Ⓐ Ⓑ Ⓒ Ⓓ
40. Ⓐ Ⓑ Ⓒ Ⓓ
41. Ⓐ Ⓑ Ⓒ Ⓓ
42. Ⓐ Ⓑ Ⓒ Ⓓ
43. Ⓐ Ⓑ Ⓒ Ⓓ
44. Ⓐ Ⓑ Ⓒ Ⓓ
45. Ⓐ Ⓑ Ⓒ Ⓓ

46. Ⓐ Ⓑ Ⓒ Ⓓ

47. Ⓐ Ⓑ Ⓒ Ⓓ

48. Ⓐ Ⓑ Ⓒ Ⓓ

49. Ⓐ Ⓑ Ⓒ Ⓓ

50. Ⓐ Ⓑ Ⓒ Ⓓ

51. Ⓐ Ⓑ Ⓒ Ⓓ

52. Ⓐ Ⓑ Ⓒ Ⓓ

53. Ⓐ Ⓑ Ⓒ Ⓓ

54. Ⓐ Ⓑ Ⓒ Ⓓ

55. Ⓐ Ⓑ Ⓒ Ⓓ

56. Ⓐ Ⓑ Ⓒ Ⓓ

57. Ⓐ Ⓑ Ⓒ Ⓓ

58. Ⓐ Ⓑ Ⓒ Ⓓ

59. Ⓐ Ⓑ Ⓒ Ⓓ

60. Ⓐ Ⓑ Ⓒ Ⓓ

FUNDAMENTALS OF COLLEGE ALGEBRA POST-TEST
72 minutes—60 questions

Directions: Carefully read each of the following 60 questions. Choose the best answer to each question and fill in the corresponding circle on the answer sheet. The Answer Key and Explanations can be found following this post-test.

1. What is the equation of a line that has an x-intercept of 8 and a slope of $\frac{2}{3}$?

    A. $y = \frac{2}{3}x + 8$

    B. $y = \frac{2}{3}x - 8$

    C. $y = \frac{2}{3}x + \frac{16}{3}$

    D. $y = \frac{2}{3}x - \frac{16}{3}$

2. What is the horizontal asymptote of the graph of $f(x) = \frac{x - 13}{x^2 - 4}$, if one exists?

    A. $y = 0$

    B. $y = -\frac{13}{4}$

    C. $y = 2$

    D. There is no horizontal asymptote.

3. The distance on a number line between a and b is 17 units. If $a = 3x + 5$ and $b = 2x + 1$, then what is a value of x?

    A. -9

    B. $-\frac{22}{3}$

    C. 8

    D. 13

4. What are the values of x if $5x^2 + 5x = -4$?

A. $-\dfrac{1}{2} - \dfrac{i}{10}\sqrt{55}$

B. $-\dfrac{1}{2} - \dfrac{1}{10}\sqrt{105}$

C. $-\dfrac{1}{2} - \dfrac{i}{2}\sqrt{3}$

D. $-\dfrac{1}{2} + \dfrac{1}{10}\sqrt{85}$

5. Simplify the expression $\dfrac{2x^3 + 8x}{4x - 16}$.

A. $\dfrac{x(x^2 + 8)}{2(x - 8)}$

B. $\dfrac{x(x^2 + 1)}{2(x - 1)}$

C. $\dfrac{x(x^2 + 4)}{2(x - 4)}$

D. $\dfrac{x(x + 4)}{2}$

6. $2x(x^2 + 4x + 8) - 6x^2(x^3 - 4) =$

A. $-6x^5 + 2x^3 + 4x + 4$

B. $-6x^5 + 2x^3 + 32x^2 + 16x$

C. $6x^5 + 2x^3 - 16x^2 + 16x$

D. $6x^5 + 2x^3 + 4x + 4$

7. Which of the following describes a relationship between a function $f(x)$ and its inverse $f^{-1}(x)$?

A. The graph of $f(x)$ is a reflection across $y = x$ of the graph of $f^{-1}(x)$.

B. The graph of $f(x)$ is a reflection across the x-axis of the graph of $f^{-1}(x)$.

C. $f^{-1}(x) = \dfrac{1}{f(x)}$

D. $(f \circ f^{-1})(x) = f(x)$

8. As x decreases, the graph of the polynomial function $f(x)$ decreases. As x increases, the graph of $f(x)$ still decreases. Which of the following could be $f(x)$?

A. $-3x^2 + 1$
B. $4x^3 + 18$
C. $-8x^5 + 2$
D. $14x^2 + 9$

9. Over what interval is $|x - 1| < 4$?

A. $(-\infty, -3) \cup (5, \infty)$
B. $(5, \infty)$
C. $(-\infty, -3)$
D. $(-3, 5)$

$$3x - y = 10$$
$$4x - 2y = 9$$

10. For the system of equations above, what is the value of x?

A. $\dfrac{19}{7}$
B. $\dfrac{11}{2}$
C. $\dfrac{13}{2}$
D. $\dfrac{19}{2}$

11. If $f(x) = \dfrac{x}{2x + 1}$, then $f^{-1}(x) =$

A. $\dfrac{2x - 1}{x}$
B. $x(2y - 1)$
C. $-y + 2xy$
D. $-\dfrac{x}{2x - 1}$

12. Multiply $(x^2 + 1)(2x^4 + 10x)$.

A. $2x(x^5 + 5)$
B. $2x(x^5 + x^3 + 5)$
C. $2x(x^5 + x^3 + 5x^2 + 5)$
D. $2x(x^5 + 2x^4 + 10x^3 + 10x)$

13. Evaluate $f(x) = 2xe^x - 4e^x$ for $4x + 1$.

    A. $8xe^{4x+1}$
    B. $2e^{4x+1}(4x - 1)$
    C. $2e^x(4x^2 - 7x - 2)$
    D. $2e^x(4x^2 - 8x + 1)$

14. Solve the following equation for u in terms of x: $1 - \log u^2 = x$

    A. $u = \sqrt{10^{1-x}}$
    B. $u = 10^{\sqrt{1-x}}$
    C. $u = 10^{\frac{1-x}{2}}$
    D. $u = 10^{2(1-x)}$

15. In terms of nonzero z_0, at which point do the lines $y = 2z_0x + 1$ and $y = 6z_0 + 5$ intersect?

    A. $\left(\dfrac{1}{z_0}, -1\right)$

    B. $\left(\dfrac{2 + 3z_0}{z_0}, 5 + 6z_0\right)$

    C. $\left(-1, -\dfrac{1}{z_0}\right)$

    D. $\left(5 + 6z_0, \dfrac{2 + 3z_0}{z_0}\right)$

16. What is the value of x if $\sqrt{5x^2 + 1} = 4x$?

    A. $x = i$

    B. $x = \sqrt{\dfrac{1}{11}}$

    C. $x = \sqrt{\dfrac{1}{21}}$

    D. $x = \dfrac{2}{5} + \dfrac{1}{5}i$

17. Simplify the numeric expression: $\dfrac{2^{-5} \cdot 4^2}{3^6}$

A. $\dfrac{512}{729}$

B. $\dfrac{1}{5,832}$

C. $\dfrac{1}{1,458}$

D. $\dfrac{128}{729}$

18. The future value A of an investment P that is continuously compounded is $A = Pe^{rt}$. How many years will it take an investment of \$5,000 to be worth \$6,000 at a continuously compounded rate of 5.1%? Round to the nearest tenth.

A. 0.4 years
B. 0.8 years
C. 1.1 years
D. 3.6 years

19. Find $(f \circ g)(x)$ when $f(x) = x^2 - 2x$ and $g(x) = \dfrac{2x}{1-x}$.

A. $\dfrac{2x^2(x-2)}{1-x}$

B. $\dfrac{4x(2x-1)}{(1-x)^2}$

C. $\dfrac{2x(x-2)}{-x^2+2x+1}$

D. $\dfrac{2x(x^2+4x-2)}{(1-x)^2}$

20. What is a solution to $4|3x-2| = a-1$ for real number a?

A. $\dfrac{-a+9}{12}$

B. $\dfrac{-a+3}{12}$

C. $\dfrac{a+1}{12}$

D. $\dfrac{3a+5}{12}$

21. Which statement is true about the function $f(x) = -2x^2 + x + 1$ over the interval $(-\infty, \infty)$?

  A. It reaches a maximum value when $x = 1$.

  B. It reaches a minimum value when $x = 1$.

  C. It reaches a maximum value when $x = \dfrac{1}{4}$.

  D. It reaches a minimum value when $x = \dfrac{1}{4}$.

22. What is the value of $f(x) = \log_2(x + 5) - 1$ for $x = 11$?

  A. $\log_2(15)$

  B. 3

  C. $\log_2(10)$

  D. 7

23. What is the vertical asymptote of the function $f(x) = \dfrac{x^2 + 3x + 2}{x^2 - 2x - 3}$?

  A. $x = -1$

  B. $x = 3$

  C. $x = -2$

  D. $x = -\dfrac{2}{3}$

$$3x - 2y = 16$$
$$-6x + 4y = a$$

24. For which value of a does the system of equations above have infinitely many solutions?

  A. -32

  B. 14

  C. -21

  D. 16

25. Which interval describes the domain of $f(x) = 2\sqrt{5-2x}$?

A. $(-\infty, \infty)$

B. $\left(-\infty, \dfrac{5}{2}\right]$

C. $\left[\dfrac{5}{2}, \infty\right)$

D. $\left[-\dfrac{5}{2}, \dfrac{5}{2}\right]$

26. For which values of x is $x^2 \leq 2$?

A. $\left[-\sqrt{2}, \sqrt{2}\,\right]$

B. $\left(-\infty, \sqrt{2}\,\right] \cup \left[\sqrt{2}, \infty\right)$

C. $[-2, 2]$

D. $\left(-\infty, 2\right] \cup \left[2, \infty\right)$

27. Astrid must save at least $500 this semester. The she has saved $200 already and will save all earnings from a job paying $12 an hour. What is the minimum number of hours Astrid must work in order to meet her savings goal?

A. 3

B. 25

C. 42

D. 59

28. Subtract: $\dfrac{2x}{4x+1} - \dfrac{x+6}{3x}$

A. $\dfrac{x-6}{x+1}$

B. $\dfrac{x-6}{(3x)(4x+1)}$

C. $\dfrac{2(x^2+3)}{(3x)(4x+1)}$

D. $\dfrac{2x^2 - 25x - 6}{(3x)(4x+1)}$

29. What is the range of $f(x) = x^2 - 6x + 1$?

A. $[-8, \infty)$

B. $(-\infty, -8]$

C. $[3, \infty)$

D. $(-\infty, 3]$

30. Simplify the compound fraction: $\dfrac{\dfrac{3x^2 + 12x}{x^2 - 3x + 2}}{\dfrac{6x^2 - 6x}{x - 2}}$

A. $\dfrac{x + 4}{2x^2 - 2x + 1}$

B. $\dfrac{x + 4}{2x^2 - 4x + 2}$

C. $\dfrac{18x^3 + 72x^2}{x^2 - 4x + 4}$

D. $\dfrac{18x^3 + 12x}{x^2 - 4x + 4}$

31. Find the value of x in terms of real number a when $2 + 2^{x+4} = a$.

A. $\log_2(a - 6)$

B. $\log_4(a) - 4$

C. $\log_4(a - 4)$

D. $\log_2(a - 2) - 4$

32. Solve the equation $\sqrt{x(x + 3)} = 2$.

A. -4

B. 1

C. -4 and 1

D. No real solutions

33. Which of the following describes the solution set to the inequality $\dfrac{3}{2}(x - 7) \geq \dfrac{4}{3}x$?

A. $x \geq -7$

B. $x \geq \dfrac{21}{2}$

C. $x \geq 42$

D. $x \geq 63$

34. What is the x-intercept of the graph of $f(x) = \frac{1}{4}x - \frac{2}{5}$?

A. $-\frac{3}{20}$

B. $\frac{1}{4}$

C. $-\frac{2}{5}$

D. $\frac{8}{5}$

35. Simplify the expression then rewrite it using radicals: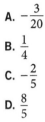

A. $\sqrt[10]{x^{37}}$

B. $\frac{1}{\sqrt[10]{x^3}}$

C. $\frac{1}{\sqrt[3]{x^{10}}}$

D. $\sqrt[37]{x^{10}}$

$$3x + 2y \geq 6$$
$$-4x + y \leq 2$$

36. Which of the following is a solution to the system of inequalities above?

A. $(0, 0)$
B. $(1, 7)$
C. $(4, 1)$
D. $(-5, 5)$

37. Completely factor the polynomial expression $2x^5 - 4x^4 + 2x^3$.

A. $2x^3(x - 1)(x + 1)$
B. $2x^3(x^2 - 4x^4 + 2x^3)$
C. $2x^3(x^2 - 2x + 1)$
D. $2x^3(x - 1)^2$

38. How many real solutions are there to the equation $x^4 - 3x^2 - 10 = 0$?

A. 0
B. 1
C. 2
D. 4

39. Solve for a in terms of b in the equation $\frac{3}{4}(a-6) = \frac{1}{2}(b+4)$.

A. $a = \frac{2}{3}(b+13)$

B. $a = \frac{2}{3}b + 10$

C. $a = \frac{2}{3}(b+20)$

D. $a = \frac{2}{3}b + \frac{13}{2}$

40. What is the conjugate of the complex number $3 + i\sqrt{5}$?

A. $3 - i\sqrt{5}$

B. $\sqrt{5} + 3i$

C. $\sqrt{5} - 3i$

D. $3 + i\sqrt{5}$

41. For which values of x does $y = 2\,|\,x - 7\,|\,-2$ lie above the x-axis?

A. $6 < x < 8$

B. $x < 6$

C. $x < 8$

D. $x < 6$ and $x > 8$

42. What is the solution set to the inequality $-3(x-4) < 17$?

A. $x > -\frac{5}{3}$

B. $x < -\frac{5}{3}$

C. $x > 7$

D. $x < 7$

43. How many turning points does the graph of $f(x) = -4x^4 + 2x^2 - 1$ have?

A. 1

B. 2

C. 3

D. 4

44. In terms of m, which of the following is a solution to the equation $x^2 + m = \sqrt{5}$?

A. $5 - 2m\sqrt{5} + m^2$

B. $\sqrt[4]{5} - \sqrt{m}$

C. $(5 - m)^{\frac{1}{2}}$

D. $\left(\sqrt{5} - m\right)^{\frac{1}{2}}$

45. In which quadrant of the Cartesian coordinate plane does the point $(-2, -5)$ lie?

A. Quadrant 1

B. Quadrant 2

C. Quadrant 3

D. Quadrant 4

46. Solve the equation for x: $\dfrac{6}{\ln(x)} = 1$

A. e^6

B. $6 - e$

C. $\dfrac{e}{6}$

D. $\dfrac{6}{e}$

47. Solve the radical equation: $\sqrt{6 - x} = x$

A. -3

B. 2

C. 2 and -3

D. No real solutions

48. Which of the following describes the solution set to the equation $\sqrt{x + 4} = \sqrt{x} - 2$?

A. All real numbers

B. One real solution

C. Two real solutions

D. No real solutions

49. Simplify the algebraic expression $2x^4 - x^3 + 4x^4 + x^3$.

    A. $6x^4$

    B. $6x^7$

    C. $6x^{14}$

    D. $6x^4 + 2x^3$

50. Solve the equation $\frac{1}{3}x + y = \frac{1}{4}z - 6y$ for x in terms of the other variables.

    A. $x = \frac{1}{12}z - \frac{7}{3}y$

    B. $x = \frac{3}{4}z - 21y$

    C. $x = \frac{1}{12}z - 7y$

    D. $x = \frac{3}{4}z - 15y$

51. Which point lies along the x-axis?

    A. $(0, 8)$

    B. $(-3, 1)$

    C. $(1, 4)$

    D. $(-1, 0)$

52. The graph of the function $f(x) = (x - 3)^2$ translates the graph of x^2

    A. up by 3 units.

    B. left by 3 units.

    C. right by 3 units.

    D. down by 3 units.

53. Simplify the algebraic expression $5x^3(x^2) - 13x^2(2x^3)$.

    A. $-21x$

    B. $-21x^5$

    C. $-21x^6$

    D. $-21x^{\frac{3}{2}}$

54. Describe the solution set to the inequality $\frac{1}{4}x - \frac{5}{6} \geq \frac{2}{3}x.$

A. $x \leq -10$

B. $x \leq -2$

C. $x \leq -\frac{5}{6}$

D. $x \leq -\frac{25}{72}$

55. Simplify the expression: $\left(\dfrac{5x^2y^4}{10xy^5}\right)^2$

A. $\dfrac{x^2}{4y^2}$

B. $\dfrac{x}{2y}$

C. $\dfrac{x^6y^{18}}{4}$

D. $\dfrac{x^3y^9}{2}$

56. Which of the following is equivalent to i^{28}?

A. -1

B. 1

C. i

D. $-i$

57. For what values of x is $x^2 > 2 + 2\sqrt{2}x$?

A. $(\sqrt{2} - 2, \sqrt{2} + 2)$

B. $(-\infty, \sqrt{2} - 2) \cup \left(\sqrt{2} + 2, \infty\right)$

C. $(32, \infty)$

D. $(-\infty, \infty)$

58. Which of the following is equivalent to $\left(\dfrac{1}{x^{-2}y^{-4}}\right)^5$?

A. $x^{10}y^{20}$

B. $\dfrac{1}{x^3y}$

C. $\sqrt[10]{x}\,\sqrt[20]{y}$

D. $\dfrac{1}{y\sqrt[3]{x}}$

59. Divide: $\dfrac{1+2i}{6-4i}$

    A. $\dfrac{1}{6} - \dfrac{1}{2}i$

    B. $-\dfrac{5}{2} - \dfrac{5}{16}i$

    C. $-\dfrac{1}{26} + \dfrac{4}{13}i$

    D. $\dfrac{5}{52}$

60. For $f(x) = \dfrac{1}{2}x^2 - 2x$ and $g(x) = \dfrac{5}{2}x^3$, find $(fg)(x)$.

    A. $\dfrac{25}{8}x^5 - 5x^3$

    B. $\dfrac{5}{4}x^5 - 5x^4$

    C. $-\dfrac{5}{2}x^3 + \dfrac{1}{2}x^2 - 2x$

    D. $\dfrac{5}{2}x^3 + \dfrac{1}{2}x^2 - 2x$

ANSWER KEY AND EXPLANATIONS

1. D	13. B	25. B	37. D	49. A
2. A	14. C	26. A	38. C	50. B
3. D	15. B	27. B	39. A	51. D
4. A	16. B	28. D	40. A	52. C
5. C	17. C	29. A	41. D	53. B
6. B	18. D	30. B	42. A	54. B
7. A	19. B	31. D	43. C	55. A
8. A	20. A	32. C	44. D	56. B
9. D	21. C	33. D	45. C	57. B
10. B	22. B	34. D	46. A	58. A
11. D	23. B	35. A	47. B	59. C
12. C	24. A	36. C	48. D	60. B

1. **The correct answer is D.** As there is an x-intercept of 8, the line passes through the point $(8, 0)$. Therefore, use the point-slope equation:

$$y - 0 = \frac{2}{3}(x - 8)$$
$$y = \frac{2}{3}x - \frac{16}{3}$$

Choice A represents a line with a y-intercept of 8, not an x-intercept. Similarly, choice B represents a line with a y-intercept of −8. You may get this answer if you have a sign error when using the point-slope formula with a y-intercept of 8. The equation in choice C is the result of a sign error when working with the point-slope formula.

2. **The correct answer is A.** To determine the horizontal asymptote, compare the degree of the numerator to the degree of the denominator. If both have the same degree, then a fraction consisting of the coefficients of the two highest degree terms is the horizontal asymptote. If the degree of the numerator is higher, then there is no horizontal asymptote. Here, the degree of the numerator is lower, which means that $y = 0$ is the horizontal asymptote. Choice B represents the y-intercept of the function. Choice C represents one of the vertical asymptotes of the function. Choice D would be correct if the degree of the numerator were higher than 2.

3. **The correct answer is D.** The distance between two values on a number line is the absolute value of their difference. Therefore,

$$\left|(3x + 5) - (2x + 1)\right| = 17$$
$$\left|x + 4\right| = 17$$

To solve this equation, write two equations and solve each for x.

$$x + 4 = 17 \Rightarrow x = 13$$
$$x + 4 = -17 \Rightarrow x = -21$$

Thus, choice D is the correct answer. Choices A and C represent solutions to $\left|2x + 1\right| = 17$. Choice B represents a solution to $\left|3x + 5\right| = 17$.

4. **The correct answer is A.** Apply the quadratic formula:

$$x = \frac{-5 - \sqrt{25 - (4)(5)(4)}}{10}$$
$$= \frac{-5 - \sqrt{-55}}{10}$$
$$= \frac{-5 - i\sqrt{55}}{10}$$
$$= -\frac{1}{2} - \frac{i}{10}\sqrt{55}$$

The statement in choice B results from using −4 in the formula; remember you must bring the −4 to the left-hand side of the equation before applying the formula. The statement in choice C results from using b in the formula instead of b^2. The statement in choice D results from making both mistakes.

5. **The correct answer is C.** Factor out common factors and cancel:

$$\frac{2x^3 + 8x}{4x - 16} = \frac{2x(x^2 + 4)}{4(x - 4)}$$
$$= \frac{x(x^2 + 4)}{2(x - 4)}$$

Choice A results from canceling common factors between 2 and 4 as the first step. These cannot be canceled; you must factor out common factors of all terms first. Choice B also results from canceling between 2 and 4, as well as canceling common factors between 8 and −16. Choice D results from treating $x^2 + 4$ (which does not factor over the real numbers) as $(x - 4)(x + 4)$.

6. **The correct answer is B.** Distribute then combine like terms:

$$2x(x^2 + 4x + 8) - 6x^2(x^3 - 4) = 2x^3 + 8x^2 + 16x - 6x^5 + 24x^2$$
$$= -6x^5 + 2x^3 + 32x^2 + 16x$$

Choice A results from only multiplying the first term in each case and not distributing. Choice C results from distributing but not including the negative sign on the second part of the expression. Choice D results from making both mistakes.

7. **The correct answer is A.** Choice A describes a property of functions and their inverses. Therefore, choice B must be incorrect. Choice C is a common mistake due to the notation. Choice D is incorrect because this operation will yield x, not $f(x)$.

8. **The correct answer is A.** For a polynomial function to have the same behavior on each end, the degree must be even, which eliminates choices B and C, which have degrees of 3 and 5, respectively. That leaves choices A and D. For a polynomial function to decrease on both sides, it must have an even degree and a negative coefficient on the highest degree term. Choice D has a positive coefficient and is therefore incorrect.

9. **The correct answer is D.** Solve the corresponding equation to get cutoffs for intervals:

$$\left|x-1\right| = 4$$

$$x - 1 = 4 \text{ or } x - 1 = -4$$

$$x = 5 \text{ or } -3$$

Check each resulting interval.

For a value less than -3, try -4:

$$\left|x-1\right| = \left|-4-1\right| = 5$$

This is larger than 4, so all values in the interval $(-\infty, -3)$ are greater than 4 and not part of the solution set (eliminating C as an answer).

For values between -3 and 5, try 0:

$$\left|x-1\right| = \left|0-1\right| = 1$$

This is less than 4, so all values in the interval $(-3, 5)$ are part of the solution set. Thus, choice D is the correct answer. There is no need to check the last interval given these answer choices.

10. **The correct answer is B.** Multiply the first equation by -2 to eliminate y:

$$
\begin{array}{r}
-6x + 2y = -20 \\
4x - 2y = 9 \\
\hline
-2x = -11 \\
x = \dfrac{11}{2}
\end{array}
$$

Choice A is the result of only multiplying $-y$ in the first equation by -2. Choice C represents the value of y. Choice D is the result of multiplying both sides of the first equation by -2.

11. **The correct answer is D.** Switch the x and y variables and solve for y.

$$f(x) = \frac{x}{2x+1}$$

$$y = \frac{x}{2x+1}$$

$$x = \frac{y}{2y+1}$$

$$y = x(2y+1)$$

$$y = 2xy + x$$

$$-x = 2xy - y$$

$$-x = y(2x-1)$$

$$y = -\frac{x}{2x-1}$$

Choice A represents the reciprocal of the function, which is a common misinterpretation of the notation for inverse functions. Choice B is the result of using the equation that comes up in the process of solving, where $y =$ is on one side. The inverse can't contain both x and y variables. Similarly, choice C is a step toward solving but is not the final answer.

12. **The correct answer is C.** Apply FOIL, since this is the product of two binomials:

$$(x^2 + 1)(2x^4 + 10x) = 2x^6 + 10x^3 + 2x^4 + 10x$$
$$= 2x^6 + 2x^4 + 10x^3 + 10x$$
$$= 2x(x^5 + x^3 + 5x^2 + 5)$$

Choices A and B are the result of only multiplying the first and last terms; choice B is also the result of multiplying the middle two terms. Choice D is the result of a simplifying error where you factored $2x$ out of the first term only but still wrote it as though it was factored out of all terms.

13. The correct answer is B. Replace each x in the expression for the function with $4x + 1$ and simplify:

$$f(4x + 1) = 2(4x + 1)e^{4x+1} - 4e^{4x+1}$$
$$= 8xe^{4x+1} + 2e^{4x+1} - 4e^{4x+1}$$
$$= 8xe^{4x+1} - 2e^{4x+1}$$
$$= 2e^{4x+1}(4x - 1)$$

Choice A is the result of not including the 1 when substituting in x in the first term. Choice C is the result of evaluating a function like you would multiplication. Choice D is the result of doing the same but not distributing.

14. The correct answer is C. Solve for u using the log rule that $\log x^p = p \log x$ and that $\log u$ is base 10:

$$1 - \log u^2 = x$$
$$-\log u^2 = x - 1$$
$$2 \log u = 1 - x$$
$$\log u = \frac{1 - x}{2}$$
$$u = 10^{\frac{1-x}{2}}$$

Choice A is the result of taking both sides to the 10th power and then applying the square root. Choice B is the result of applying the square root once the log was isolated. Choice D is the result of taking both sides to the 10th power as a first step, instead of when log is isolated.

15. The correct answer is B. Set the equations equal and solve for x as the first step. This will give the x-coordinate of the intersection point:

$$2z_0 x + 1 = 6z_0 + 5$$
$$2z_0 x - 6z_0 = 4$$
$$2z_0(x - 3) = 4$$
$$x - 3 = \frac{4}{2z_0} = \frac{2}{z_0}$$
$$x = \frac{2}{z_0} + 3 = \frac{2 + 3z_0}{z_0}$$

Verify your answer by substituting x into either equation to get the y-coordinate. Choices A and C are the result of combining the unlike terms $6z_0$ and $2z_0x$; choice D is the result of mixing up the coordinates.

16. **The correct answer is B.** Square both sides and then solve for x:

$$\sqrt{5x^2 + 1} = 4x$$
$$5x^2 + 1 = 16x^2$$
$$-11x^2 = -1$$
$$x = -\sqrt{\frac{1}{11}}$$

There are two answer choices, and typically you would check both, as there can be extraneous solutions. However, only one is listed, so the correct answer must be choice B. In fact, if you were to check $x = -\sqrt{\frac{1}{11}}$, you would find it is extraneous.

Choice A is the result of dropping the square root and solving the resulting equation. Choice C is the result of correctly squaring both sides but then adding $5x^2$ and $16x^2$ when solving. Choice D is the result of squaring only the left-hand side of the equation.

17. **The correct answer is C.** Recall that exponents with the same base, when multiplied, result in an exponent that is the sum of the original exponents and that $x^{-1} = \frac{1}{x}$ for nonzero values:

$$\frac{2^{-5} \cdot 4^2}{3^6} = \frac{2^{-5} \cdot 2^4}{3^6}$$
$$= \frac{2^{-1}}{3^6}$$
$$= \frac{1}{2(729)}$$
$$= \frac{1}{1,458}$$

Choice A is the result of calculating without the negative sign. Choice B is the result of adding exponents even though they have different bases. Choice D is the combination of both mistakes.

18. **The correct answer is D.** Substitute values into the equation and solve for x. Recall that $\ln(x)$ is the inverse of e^x:

$$A = Pe^{rt}$$

$$6{,}000 = 5{,}000e^{0.051t}$$

$$\frac{6}{5} = e^{0.051t}$$

$$\ln\left(\frac{6}{5}\right) = 0.051t$$

$$\frac{\ln\left(\frac{6}{5}\right)}{0.051} = t$$

$$t = 3.6$$

Choice A is the result of using 0.51 instead of 0.051. Recall that percentages are over 100. Choice B results from mixing up 6,000 and 5,000 and just dividing by $e^{0.051}$ when solving. Choice C is the result of just dividing by $e^{0.051}$.

19. **The correct answer is B.** This is a composition of functions. This is equivalent to $f(g(x))$. Thus, replace each x in the first function with the expression defining the second function:

$$f(g(x)) = (g(x))^2 - 2(g(x))$$

$$= \left(\frac{2x}{1-x}\right)^2 - 2\left(\frac{2x}{1-x}\right)$$

$$= \frac{4x^2}{(1-x)^2} - \frac{4x}{1-x}$$

Now multiply the numerator and denominator of the second fraction by $1-x$ to add the two fractions:

$$\frac{4x^2}{(1-x)^2} - \frac{4x}{1-x} = \frac{4x^2}{(1-x)^2} - \frac{4x(1-x)}{(1-x)^2}$$

$$= \frac{4x^2 - 4x + 4x^2}{(1-x)^2}$$

$$= \frac{8x^2 - 4x}{(1-x)^2}$$

$$= \frac{4x(2x-1)}{(1-x)^2}$$

Choice A results from treating the substitution as multiplication for the two functions. Choice C represents $g(f(x))$. Choice D results from not substituting in the $2x$ term.

20. **The correct answer is A.** Isolate the absolute value and write two equations, solving each for x:

$$\left|3x - 2\right| = \frac{a-1}{4}$$

Equation 1:

$$3x - 2 = \frac{a-1}{4}$$

$$3x = \frac{a-1}{4} + 2$$

$$3x = \frac{a+7}{4}$$

$$x = \frac{a+7}{12}$$

Equation 2:

$$3x - 2 = -\frac{a-1}{4}$$

$$3x = \frac{-(a-1)}{4} + 2$$

$$3x = \frac{-a+9}{4}$$

$$x = \frac{-a+9}{12}$$

Choice B results from distributing the 4 into the absolute value and only multiplying the first term. Choice C is the other solution resulting from this mistake. Choice D results from only dividing 2 by 3 in the last step of solving the linear equation in equation 1.

21. **The correct answer is C.** The function given has a graph that is a parabola opening downward because the squared term has a negative coefficient. Over that interval, the function reaches a maximum value, eliminating choices B and D.

The x value where this maximum is reached is found using the formula $x = -\dfrac{b}{2a}$. In this case,

$$x = -\frac{b}{2a} = -\frac{1}{2(-2)} = \frac{1}{4}$$

22. **The correct answer is B.** Substitute 11 in for x and evaluate:

$$\begin{aligned}
f(11) &= \log_2(11+5) - 1 \\
&= \log_2(16) - 1 \\
&= 4 - 1 \\
&= 3
\end{aligned}$$

Choice A results from subtracting the 1 from the 16 inside the log. You can't bring terms outside of the log into the log before evaluating. Choice C results from the same mistake but also forgetting to add 5. Choice D results from dividing 16 by 2 when evaluating $\log_2(16)$.

23. **The correct answer is B.** First, factor. An asymptote is any value that makes the denominator 0 but does not make the numerator 0. Thus, you must cancel any common factors when determining the equation of a vertical asymptote:

$$\frac{x^2 + 3x + 2}{x^2 - 2x - 3} = \frac{(x+1)(x+2)}{(x+1)(x-3)} = \frac{x+2}{x-3}$$

Choice A would represent a vertical asymptote if the numerator did not have the factor $x + 1$. Choice C is the result of using a zero for the numerator instead of the denominator. Choice D represents the y-intercept of the function.

24. **The correct answer is A.** Systems of equations have infinitely many solutions when the two equations represent the same line. Notice that the left side of equation 2 is the left side of equation 1 multiplied by –2. To make this represent the same line, 16 must also be multiplied by –2, giving –32. All other choices will result in a system with no solution.

25. The correct answer is B. The square root must be nonnegative. For this reason, set up an inequality to find values that satisfy this condition:

$$5 - 2x \geq 0$$
$$-2x \geq -5$$
$$x \leq \frac{5}{2}$$

This is represented by the interval in choice B. All values smaller than or equal to $\frac{5}{2}$. Choice A represents all real numbers, but this cannot be correct as the values in the radical cannot be negative. Choice C is the result of not flipping the inequality when solving. Choice D is from misunderstanding the result of the inequality as meaning all values between $-\frac{5}{2}$ and $\frac{5}{2}$.

26. The correct answer is A. We can view this inequality as $x^2 - 2 \leq 0$. The graph of $y = x^2 - 2$ is a parabola opening upwards. Therefore, the graph will be above the x-axis to the right and left of the x-intercepts and below between. So, the x-intercepts must be determined. This can be done by solving the equivalent equation:

$$x^2 = 2$$
$$x = -\sqrt{2}$$

Choice B represents intervals where the graph is above the x-axis and thus positive. Choices C and D result from using intercepts of 2, having not taken the square root when determining intercepts.

27. The correct answer is B. Let h represent the number of hours. Then you can write the inequality $200 + 12h \geq 500$ since Astrid has already saved $200 (fixed) and is working for $12 an hour (depends on hours). "At least" indicates greater than or equal to. Now, solve the inequality:

$$200 + 12h \geq 500$$
$$12h \geq 300$$
$$h \geq 25$$

Therefore, she must work at least 25 hours. Choice A results from writing $200h + 12 \geq 500$ and solving this inequality. Choice C results from not including the $200 already saved. Choice D results from including the $200 saved in the wrong part of the inequality—that is, writing and solving $12x \geq 700$.

28. **The correct answer is D.** The common denominator is $(3x)(4x + 1)$. Multiply both the numerator and denominator of the first fraction by $3x$ and the second by $4x + 1$. Then, you can subtract:

$$\frac{2x}{4x+1} - \frac{x+6}{3x} = \frac{2x(3x)}{(3x)(4x+1)} - \frac{(x+6)(4x+1)}{(3x)(4x+1)}$$
$$= \frac{6x^2 - 4x^2 - 25x - 6}{(3x)(4x+1)}$$
$$= \frac{2x^2 - 25x - 6}{(3x)(4x+1)}$$

Choice A results from subtracting across on both the numerator and denominator. Choice B results from subtracting across on the numerators and finding a common denominator by only multiplying the denominator by the correct value. Choice C results from not using FOIL after finding a common denominator in the first step.

29. **The correct answer is A.** The graph of this function is a parabola opening up. Therefore, it reaches a minimum y value and increases to infinity from there (choices B and D). To find the x value where this minimum occurs, use the formula to find the vertex:

$$-\frac{b}{2a} = \frac{6}{2} = 3$$

Choice C uses this value, but that is incorrect. For the range, you must use the corresponding y value. To find this, evaluate the function for 3:

$$f(3) = 3^2 - 6(3) + 1 = -8$$

30. The correct answer is B. Write the compound fraction as a division problem and then "flip and multiply." To "flip and multiply," keep the first fraction the same but then multiply it by the reciprocal of the second fraction:

$$\frac{\dfrac{3x^2+12x}{x^2-3x+2}}{\dfrac{6x^2-6x}{x-2}} = \frac{3x^2+12x}{x^2-3x+2} \div \frac{6x^2-6x}{x-2}$$

$$= \frac{3x^2+12x}{x^2-3x+2} \times \frac{x-2}{6x^2-6x}$$

$$= \frac{3x(x+4)}{(x-2)(x-1)} \times \frac{x-2}{6x(x-1)}$$

$$= \frac{x+4}{x-1} \times \frac{1}{2(x-1)}$$

$$= \frac{x+4}{2(x^2-2x+1)}$$

$$= \frac{x+4}{2x^2-4x+2}$$

Choice A is the result of correctly performing the steps but not distributing the 2 in the denominator to all terms. Choice C is the product of the two fractions. Choice D is the product of the two fractions with a distributing mistake in the numerator.

31. The correct answer is D. Recall that $\log_2(x)$ is the inverse of the function 2^x. Therefore, isolate the exponential term and take log base 2 of both sides:

$$2+2^{x+4} = a$$

$$2^{x+4} = a-2$$

$$\log_2(2^{x+4}) = \log_2(a-2)$$

$$x+4 = \log_2(a-2)$$

$$x = \log_2(a-2)-4$$

Choice A results from subtracting the 4 from the inside the log function. Choice B results from adding the 2s on the left before taking the log base 4. Choice C results from doing the same but also subtracting 4 from the inside of the function.

32. **The correct answer is C.** Square both sides and then solve the resulting equations. Check each answer to verify that it is not an extraneous solution:

$$\sqrt{x(x+3)} = 2$$
$$x(x+3) = 4$$
$$x^2 + 3x = 4$$
$$x^2 + 3x - 4 = 0$$
$$(x+4)(x-1) = 0$$

Therefore, the possible solutions are -4 and 1.

Check each possible solution, starting with $x = -4$:

$$\sqrt{-4(-4+3)} = 2$$
$$\sqrt{-4(-1)} = 2$$

This is a true statement, so we have one solution so far.

We still need to test 1. Check $x = 1$:

$$\sqrt{1(1+3)} = 2$$
$$\sqrt{1(4)} = 2$$

This is also a true statement, so we have two real solutions. The other choices are not correct as they don't include the two real solutions.

33. **The correct answer is D.** Distribute and solve the inequality as you would a linear equation:

$$\frac{3}{2}(x-7) \geq \frac{4}{3}x$$
$$\frac{3}{2}x - \frac{21}{2} \geq \frac{4}{3}x$$
$$\frac{3}{2}x - \frac{4}{3}x \geq \frac{21}{2}$$
$$\frac{1}{6}x \geq \frac{21}{2}$$
$$x \geq 63$$

Choice A results from not distributing on the left and subtracting fractions across. To subtract fractions, find a common denominator. Choice B results from only subtracting the fractions across, and choice C results from not distributing.

34. The correct answer is D. The x-intercept is the value of x when y = 0. So set y = 0 and solve:

$$f(x) = \frac{1}{4}x - \frac{2}{5}$$
$$y = \frac{1}{4}x - \frac{2}{5}$$
$$0 = \frac{1}{4}x - \frac{2}{5}$$
$$\frac{2}{5} = \frac{1}{4}x$$
$$\frac{8}{5} = x$$

Choice A results from evaluating the function at x = 1. Choice B represents the slope of the function, and choice C represents the y-intercept of the function.

35. The correct answer is A. Apply the laws of exponents and the fact that $x^{\frac{m}{n}} = \sqrt[n]{x^m}$:

$$\frac{x^{\frac{1}{5}} \cdot x^2}{x^{-2} \cdot x^{\frac{1}{2}}} = \frac{x^{\frac{11}{5}}}{x^{-\frac{3}{2}}} = x^{\frac{11}{5} - \left(-\frac{3}{2}\right)} = x^{\frac{37}{10}} = \sqrt[10]{x^{37}}$$

Choice B results from canceling the x^2 and x^{-2}. These are different terms, so they can't be canceled. Choice C results from making the same mistake and mixing up how to write a radical. Choice D results from confusion on how to write a radical.

36. The correct answer is C. A solution must work for both inequalities. The fastest way to solve this problem is to try each ordered pair in both given inequalities. Checking, you will find that x = 4 and y = 1, making each inequality a true statement. Choices A and D do not work for either inequality. Choice B works only for the first inequality.

37. The correct answer is D. Factor out common factors, then factor the resulting quadratic. The common factor is $2x^3$:

$$2x^5 - 4x^4 + 2x^3 = 2x^3(x^2 - 2x + 1)$$
$$= 2x^3(x-1)(x-1)$$
$$= 2x^3(x-1)^2$$

Choice A is the result of factoring $x^2 - 2x + 1$ as $(x-1)(x+1)$. Choice B is the result of factoring the common factor out of only the first term. You must factor it out from all terms. Choice C is not completely factored, since the quadratic can be factored over the real numbers.

38. The correct answer is C. The maximum number of real solutions is the same as the degree of the polynomial, which is 4 here. Therefore, it is possible that choice D is an answer. Any of the other answers may be true, however, so the equation must be solved. Note that the equation is in quadratic form:

$$x^4 - 3x^2 - 10 = 0$$
$$(x^2)^2 - 3x^2 - 10 = 0$$
$$\left(x^2 - 5\right)\left(x^2 + 2\right) = 0$$

This yields two real solutions, as the solutions are $\pm\sqrt{5}$ and $\pm i\sqrt{2}$. Remember that solutions with i are not real numbers. Thus, only answer choice C is correct.

39. The correct answer is A. Distribute and solve as you would a normal linear equation. Be sure to solve for a and not b:

$$\frac{3}{4}(a-6) = \frac{1}{2}(b+4)$$

$$\frac{3}{4}a - \frac{18}{4} = \frac{1}{2}b + \frac{4}{2}$$

$$\frac{3}{4}a = \frac{1}{2}b + \frac{4}{2} + \frac{18}{4}$$

$$\frac{3}{4}a = \frac{1}{2}b + \frac{26}{4}$$

$$\frac{3}{4}a = \frac{1}{2}b + \frac{13}{2}$$

$$\frac{3}{4}a = \frac{1}{2}(b+13)$$

$$a = \frac{4}{6}(b+13)$$

$$a = \frac{2}{3}(b+13)$$

Choice B is the result of not distributing the first term to all terms in the first step and multiplying both sides by $\frac{3}{4}$ instead of $\frac{4}{3}$ when solving. Choice C is the result of the distributing mistake, and choice D is the result of the multiplication mistake.

40. The correct answer is A. The conjugate repeats the complex number but changes the middle sign. A complex number is not its own conjugate; therefore, choice D is incorrect. You do not switch terms, so choices B and C are incorrect.

41. The correct answer is D. A function lies above the x-axis when $y > 0$. Therefore, we must solve the equation $0 = 2|x-7|-2$ and then apply this to the inequality $2|x-7|-2 > 0$:

$$0 = 2|x-7|-2$$
$$2 = 2|x-7|$$
$$1 = |x-7|$$

This yields two equations: $x - 7 = 1$ and $x - 7 = -1$. These have solutions 8 and 6, respectively. You could now use test points; however, recall that the graph of an absolute value function is a V shape and opens upward if the coefficient of the absolute value is positive. So, this graph opens upward and hits the x-axis at 8 and 6. By the shape, we know it is above the x-axis for values smaller than 6 and larger than 8, so choice D is the only correct answer.

42. **The correct answer is A.** Solve the inequality just as you would a linear equation. Remember that when you divide or multiply by a negative value, the inequality sign "flips":

$$-3(x - 4) < 17$$
$$-3x + 12 < 17$$
$$-3x < 5$$
$$x > -\frac{5}{3}$$

Choice B is the result of forgetting to flip the inequality. Choice C is the result of not distributing -3 to all terms; choice D is also the result of this same mistake, as well as not flipping the inequality.

43. **The correct answer is C.** A polynomial function always has $n - 1$ turning points where n is the degree. Here, the degree is 4, so there are 3 turning points.

44. **The correct answer is D.** Isolate the squared term and apply the square root rule. Note that roots do not distribute over addition or subtraction. Also remember that taking the square root is the same as taking an expression to the half power:

$$x^2 + m = \sqrt{5}$$
$$x^2 = \sqrt{5} - m$$
$$x = -\sqrt{\sqrt{5} - m}$$
$$x = -\left(\sqrt{5} - m\right)^{\frac{1}{2}}$$

Choice A is the result of isolating the squared term but then squaring both sides to solve. Choice B is the result of breaking up the square root over addition. Choice C is the result of treating $\sqrt{\sqrt{5}}$ as 5 when it is actually $\sqrt[4]{5}$.

45. **The correct answer is C.** Points in quadrant 4 have positive x-coordinates and negative y-coordinates. In quadrant 1, both coordinates are positive. In quadrant 2, the x-coordinate is negative while the y-coordinate is positive. In quadrant 3, both coordinates are negative.

46. **The correct answer is A.** Solve, recalling that the $\ln(x)$ is log base e of x:

$$\frac{6}{\ln(x)} = 1$$
$$\ln(x) = 6$$
$$x = e^6$$

Choice B is the result of treating this as though it were $\ln(6)$ and applying the incorrect rule that this would simplify to $\ln(6 - x)$. Choice C results from treating the left-hand side as equivalent to $\ln(6x)$, and choice D is the result of treating the left-hand side as equivalent to $\ln\left(\frac{6}{x}\right)$.

47. **The correct answer is B.** Solve by squaring both sides. Check the answers for extraneous solutions:

$$\sqrt{6-x} = x$$
$$6 - x = x^2$$
$$0 = x^2 + x - 6$$
$$0 = (x + 3)(x - 2)$$
$$x = -3, 2$$

Checking –3, $\sqrt{6-(-3)} = \sqrt{9}$, which is not equal to –3, –3 is not a solution. Checking 2, $\sqrt{6-2} = \sqrt{4}$. This is equal to 2, so 2 is the only solution.

48. The correct answer is D. Solve by squaring both sides. Check the answers for extraneous solutions:

$$\sqrt{x+4} = \sqrt{x} - 2$$
$$x + 4 = x - 4\sqrt{x} + 4$$
$$0 = -4\sqrt{x}$$
$$x = 0$$

Checking 0, the left-hand side of the equation yields 2, while the right-hand side of the equation yields −2. Thus, there are no real solutions to this equation.

49. The correct answer is A. Combine like terms, which are terms with the same variable and the same coefficient:

$$2x^4 - x^3 + 4x^4 + x^3 = (2x^4 + 4x^4) + (-x^3 + x^3) = 6x^4$$

Choice B is the result of adding the exponents on the left and on the right. You add exponents only when multiplying terms with the same base. Choice C is similar, except all exponents were added. Choice D is the result of missing the negative sign on the x^3 term.

50. The correct answer is B. Solve as usual, treating the other variables as you would constants in the equation (though you cannot combine them):

$$\frac{1}{3}x + y = \frac{1}{4}z - 6y$$
$$\frac{1}{3}x = \frac{1}{4}z - 7y$$
$$x = \frac{3}{4}z - 21y$$

Choice A is the result of multiplying both sides by $\frac{1}{3}$ instead of 3 in the last step. Choice C is the result of doing this but only multiplying the first term. In choice D, you mistakenly added y to both sides instead of subtracting.

51. The correct answer is D. Points along the x-axis have no vertical "height." Thus, their y-coordinate is 0. This means choice D is correct. Note that choice A lies along the y-axis.

52. The correct answer is C. For any function, a translation of a graph k units to the right is represented by $f(x - k)$. Thus, choice C must be the correct answer.

53. The correct answer is B. Multiply and combine like terms. Recall that when you multiply terms with the same base, you add exponents and multiply the coefficients:

$$5x^3(x^2) - 13x^2(2x^3) = 5x^5 - 26x^5 = -21x^5$$

Choice A is the result of subtracting exponents. Choice C is the result of multiplying exponents. Choice D is the result of dividing exponents.

54. The correct answer is B. Solve as you would a linear equation, but remember to "flip" the sign of the inequality when dividing or multiplying by a negative:

$$\frac{1}{4}x - \frac{5}{6} \geq \frac{2}{3}x$$
$$\frac{3}{12}x - \frac{8}{12}x \geq \frac{5}{6}$$
$$-\frac{5}{12}x \geq \frac{5}{6}$$
$$-5x \geq 10$$
$$x \leq -2$$

Choice A is the result of finding a common denominator but not multiplying numerators by the correct values before subtracting fractions. Choice C is the result of subtracting the fractions across. Choice D is the result of multiplying both sides by $-\frac{5}{12}$ instead of its reciprocal.

55. The correct answer is A. Apply the rules of exponents. When dividing exponents with the same base, subtract exponents. When taking a power to a power, multiply. Powers outside of fractions will affect every term in the fraction:

$$\left(\frac{5x^2y^4}{10xy^5}\right)^2 = \left(\frac{x}{2y}\right)^2 = \frac{x^2}{4y^2}$$

Choice B is incorrect because the result was not squared. Choice C is the result of adding exponents instead of subtracting, and choice D is the result of adding exponents and not squaring.

56. The correct answer is B. Apply the rules of exponents and the following rules:

$$i^2 = -1$$
$$i^3 = -i$$
$$i^4 = 1$$

For this problem,

$$i^{28} = (i^4)^7 = 1$$

57. The correct answer is B. Bring all terms to one side and solve the resulting quadratic. You can then test intervals or make a conclusion based on the results:

$$x^2 = 2 + 2\sqrt{2}x$$
$$x^2 - 2\sqrt{2}x - 2 = 0$$

Apply the quadratic formula:

$$\frac{-(-2\sqrt{2}) \pm \sqrt{(2\sqrt{2})^2 - 4(1)(-2)}}{2} = \frac{2\sqrt{2} \pm \sqrt{8+8}}{2} = \frac{2\sqrt{2} \pm \sqrt{16}}{2} = \sqrt{2} \pm 2$$

You could now use test points, but recall that this is a quadratic opening upward (positive coefficient on the squared term) that has two x-intercepts. The parabola will be below the x-axis (negative) between these values and above it (positive) outside of these values. The corresponding inequality is $x^2 - 2\sqrt{2}x - 2 > 0$, so it is above the x-axis outside of these values.

Choice A represents where the function lies below the x-axis. Choice C is the result if you drop the x from $2\sqrt{2}$. Choice D would be correct if there were only one x-intercept.

58. **The correct answer is A.** Recall that $x^{-n} = \dfrac{1}{x^n}$ and that you multiply when taking a power to a power. The first rule can be interpreted as moving a negative exponent term in the denominator to the numerator and vice-versa:

$$\left(\frac{1}{x^{-2}y^{-4}}\right)^5 = \left(x^2y^4\right)^5 = x^{10}y^{20}$$

Choice B is the result of adding exponents instead of multiplying when taking a power to a power. Choice C is the result of treating negative exponents like radicals; the expression in choice D is similar, but you also incorrectly added the exponents.

59. **The correct answer is C.** To divide complex numbers, multiply both the numerator and denominator by the conjugate of the denominator:

$$\frac{1+2i}{6-4i}\left(\frac{6+4i}{6+4i}\right) = \frac{6+16i-8}{36+16} = \frac{-2+16i}{52} = -\frac{1}{26}+\frac{4}{13}i$$

Choice A is the result of splitting the original fraction in two separate fractions and reducing. This is not a valid mathematical operation with fractions. Choice B is the result of using the conjugate of the numerator. Choice D is the result of using the conjugate of the numerator on the numerator and the conjugate of the denominator on the denominator.

60. **The correct answer is B.** The notation given asks you to multiply the two functions. Therefore,

$$(fg)(x) = \left(\frac{1}{2}x^2 - 2x\right)\left(\frac{5}{2}x^3\right) = \frac{5}{4}x^5 - 5x^4$$

Choice A represents the composition of the two functions. Choice C represents the difference of the two functions, and choice D is the sum of the two functions.

Like what you see? Get unlimited access to Peterson's full catalog of DSST practice tests, instructional videos, flashcards and more for **75% off the first month!** Go to **www.petersons.com/testprep/dsst** and use coupon code **DSST2020** at checkout. Offer expires July 1, 2021.

CPSIA information can be obtained
at www.ICGtesting.com
Printed in the USA
JSHW042125200722
28277JS00012B/141